OUT-OF-WEDLOCK
BIRTHS

OUT-OF-WEDLOCK BIRTHS

The United States in Comparative Perspective

Mark Abrahamson

Westport, Connecticut
London

Library of Congress Cataloging-in-Publication Data

Abrahamson, Mark.
    Out-of-wedlock births : the United States in comparative
perspective / Mark Abrahamson.
        p.   cm.
    Includes bibliographical references and index.
    ISBN 0–275–95662–8 (alk. paper).—ISBN 0–275–95665–2 (pbk. :
alk. paper)
    1. Unmarried mothers—United States.   2. Unmarried mothers—
History.   3. Illegitimate births—United States.   4. Middle class
women—United States.   5. Working class women—United States.
6. Minority women—United States.   I. Title.
HV700.5.A27   1998
306.874'3'09—DC21   97–43954

British Library Cataloguing in Publication Data is available.

Library of Congress Catalog Card Number: 97–43954
ISBN: 0–275–95662–8
        0–275–95665–2 (pbk.)

First published in 1998

Praeger Publishers, 88 Post Road West, Westport, CT 06881
An imprint of Greenwood Publishing Group, Inc.

Printed in the United States of America

The paper used in this book complies with the
Permanent Paper Standard issued by the National
Information Standards Organization (Z39.48–1984).

10 9 8 7 6 5 4 3 2 1

Contents

Preface

Over the last several decades I have been watching, with dismay, the deterioration of social life in most of America's inner cities. The poverty, school failures, crime, and violence that are now pervasive in the urban core all seem to have been markedly worsened by the increase in the number of young women who had babies despite not having husbands. As I began to pay more attention to the issue, I was struck by the ideological and philosophical differences separating analysts on the Left and the Right. While agreeing that nonmarital childbearing has exacerbated many inner-city problems, they disagreed completely on whether it was a cause, a symptom, or an effect. I wondered if I could steer a middle course and bring a more diverse set of data to bear on the question.

It also became clear to me that young, inner-city black and Hispanic women were the stereotypical unwed mothers and that while a significant portion of unwed mothers did fit this description, many did not. Older and wealthier women were also having children outside of marriage because, as conventionally defined, marriage simply did not fit their lifestyles. I was intrigued with the variability of the women who were having children outside of marriage, and I wondered if it was possible to generalize about this demographic category and about the social conditions associated with fluctuations in its relative size.

I initially began to assemble data on a couple of dozen places that, at different time periods, experienced increases in out-of-wedlock births. This produced chapters that contained little "snippets" that, in three or four pages, provided condensed pictures of out-of-wedlock birth patterns and related variables in a variety of places. However, my volunteer readers did not find this presentation very meaningful. Any conclusions seemed arbitrary because the description of each place was too brief. Further, I could not find adequate data on enough places to produce a sample from which one could really generalize. I concluded then that fuller descriptions of a small number of well-selected case studies was a better approach, and the reader will see the result.

I am grateful to a great many scholars who were kind enough to share copies of their unpublished works with me. I benefited enormously from having access to this material. I owe a special debt to Frank Reeves, who creatively designed the three illustrations that appear in the middle chapters. My wife Marlene was a supportive reader, and I thank her for giving me much encouragement.

PART 1

BACKGROUND AND THE CONTEMPORARY UNITED STATES

Part 1 of this book is primarily devoted to an examination of the contemporary United States, though it also introduces many of the terms and concepts that will be employed throughout the book in describing diverse societies. Chapter 1 describes the women, rich and poor, young and old, who have recently had children outside of marriage, and then poses some basic questions about the universal nature of marriage, how it is related to parenthood, and how the status of offspring is dependent upon the status of their parents. This chapter also presents a theoretical perspective on the influence of social institutions upon people's lives, a perspective that will inform our analyses of the contemporary United States as well as our analyses of other times and places.

Chapter 2 focuses upon current out-of-wedlock birth rates and ratios in the United States. It shows how much more frequent such births have become among black, Hispanic, and white women over the past twenty or thirty years. This chapter also describes the principal sources of data for studying out-of-wedlock births and related phenomena in the United States: census reports, vital statistics records, and longitudinal surveys. The chapter also examines the kinds of biases that can distort the figures provided by any of these three major sources of data.

In chapter 3 nonmarital births are viewed as the last step in a chain of events that begins when people engage in sexual intercourse prior to or outside of marriage. The intervening steps involve not using contraception or abortion and not defining pregnancy as a signal to marry. Trends pertaining to each of the steps in this chain are reviewed in order to make clear how the different components have contributed to the overall increase in

out-of-wedlock births. In addition, this chapter describes the distinguishing characteristics of the parents of children born out of
wedlock, though a lot more information is available for mothers
than for fathers.

1
Marriage and Parenthood

Over the past several decades there has been a marked increase in the percentage of all infants born to women who were neither married at the time of their births nor likely to marry soon after. The women whose births have contributed to this trend are very diverse. A growing percentage of out-of-wedlock births involve "older" (i.e., over 35 years of age) career women. Some of them have such an engulfing commitment to their occupations that they are left with little time or energy to date or try to find a husband. Still other women follow sexual lifestyles in which a conventional marriage has no place. The family situation to which these women aspire does not include a husband/father or any other male surrogate to whom they have a serious and continuing attachment. In any case, as some of these women approach age 40, they fear that their biological capacities to bear children will soon come to an end, and they then decide to try to become pregnant before it is too late.

MADONNA AND MURPHY BROWN

Madonna was one of a long line of celebrities who fit the description of the single mother just presented. At age 36, in 1995, she publicly declared that she desperately wanted a child but that marriage was not part of the picture she envisioned. In the spring of 1996, Madonna's publicist announced that the 37-year-old star finally had that maternal glow: "Her eyes look very sparkly."[1] The father? He was disclosed as an employee, her 29-year-old personal trainer. Despite Madonna's pregnancy, the couple have no plans to marry, and that announcement was not met by public criticism. Maybe by 1996 no one cared anymore. Or perhaps because it was Madonna, conventional morality did not seem to apply.

The most famous single mother of this type is probably the fictitious television character Murphy Brown, and when the script called for her to become a single mom, it certainly did attract criticism. Candice Bergen starred in this sitcom about a single woman pursuing a career as a television reporter. The name of the series was the name of the fictitious character. The notoriety arose when, during the 1992 season, the show's producers decided that as part of the television series, Murphy Brown would have a child out of wedlock. The then vice president of the United States, Dan Quayle, furiously condemned the fictitious character's decision as celebrating a breakdown of family life in America. He blamed Hollywood for promoting antifamily messages, and said it reflected a "poverty of values" responsible for a myriad of social problems, including welfare cheats, rioters, and looters.[2]

Murphy Brown's decision to have a child while single raised a number of fundamental questions. However, in many respects it also led to a digression from some of the core issues, because the television character was a mature woman of reasonable economic means. And while the proportion of Murphy Brown–type single mothers has increased, older professional women still comprise a small percentage of all unmarried mothers. More typical is the younger woman, in her early twenties or still in her teens. Many of them are only marginally able to support themselves *without* a child, and the additional dependent creates serious difficulties for them. When these younger women do not marry their children's fathers, it is either because the man also lacks the economic resources necessary for the couple to establish their own household or because the man or woman does not view their procreative liaison as implying a more permanent and diffuse relationship.

YOUNG AND POOR

Young single mothers frequently need a great deal of help and economic assistance in caring for their children. Unfortunately, many cannot get all the help they need, and life becomes extremely difficult for both these young mothers and their children. The most publicized cases arise when the youngsters are found to be neglected or abused and reporters and experts ask what went wrong to permit such problems to occur. Consider, as illustrative, the situation of Ernestine Pallet. By age 16 she had left school and begun working at an unskilled service job. She lived with an aunt, but the two of them never had a close relationship.

Then she met Eugene, 22 years old at the time, and "zing went the strings of her heart." It did not matter to Ernestine that he had a bad reputation in her aunt's neighborhood. He was known to be a gambler, he tended to drink too much alcohol, and when he was drunk he was especially likely to get into fights, either with his fists or a knife. In addition, the neighbors considered him a lazy and shiftless young man because he did not regularly hold a job. None of this discouraged Ernestine, and she resented her aunt's criticism of him. She got so tired of the hassle her aunt gave her every time she went out with Eugene that she left home, moved in with him, and worked to support them both.

In a few months she was pregnant, and at age 17 gave birth to a son. She dutifully obeyed Eugene's wishes, returning to work as quickly as possible after the birth of their son. She did very much want for them to marry, but he scoffed at the idea. She kept asking him, but gently, because when he felt she was nagging him, he usually punched her into silence. He continued to drink and gamble, working occasionally and mostly living off Ernestine for the next two years. Then one day he took everything of value in their apartment, including every bit of the food, and simply took off, leaving her in a confused daze. She sought public assistance, but the officials told her it would take eight days to conduct the proper investigation of her needs and resources, and they refused to provide any help in the interim. Frightened and confused, unsure where to turn, she took her crying, hungry child back to her apartment and strangled it to death. In order to conceal her actions, she subsequently told everyone who inquired about the little boy that she had to place him in an institution.

Believe it or not, when Eugene suddenly appeared at the door a few months later, she welcomed him back, and each of them soon resumed their former roles. Ernestine again took his physical and emotional abuse, but when she discovered she was pregnant again, she became desperate for a way out of the situation. Frantic, she finally walked into a local police station and confessed to murdering her child. The authorities found her story plausible from the very beginning, because in Ernestine and Eugene's neighborhood there had recently been a large number of infants abandoned in alleys and doorways, and a good number of them had died by the time people found them. The police took her into custody, and she soon went to trial, was convicted, and served five years in prison.

Many features of Ernestine's situation will sound very familiar to contemporary Americans: a young woman with limited schooling, a poor home situation, and a dead-end service job becomes pregnant without marrying, and then she and her child confront every kind of problem imaginable. In fact, however, Ernestine and Eugene—an actual, not fictitious, couple—spent their entire lives in Paris, France, and the year in which they first moved in together was 1878.[3]

In later chapters of this book we will examine out-of-wedlock births in other places and other times, and find analogues to both Ernestine Pallet and Murphy Brown. Our most immediate task is to begin to examine the major concepts that we will need to employ in an analysis of out-of-wedlock births. The most pertinent are parenthood and marriage, and they must be clearly understood before all the implications of out-of-wedlock births are fully comprehensible. At first glance, parenthood and marriage each imply a distinct social status; that is, one is or is not married, and one is or is not a parent. That is often the case, but as we will see, under many circumstances marriage and parenthood statuses can be ambiguous, and a resolution can require negotiations among the people who are involved.

SEX AND PROCREATION: MALINOWSKI'S VIEW

After analyzing marital patterns in many different preliterate societies, the social anthropologist Bronislaw Malinowski concluded that marriage as a universal practice could best be defined as a contract that provided a couple with "a license" to be parents. Writing in the 1920s and 1930s, he noted that there were societies in which women were expected to be virgins when they married and that if one took a sample of only these societies, one would likely conclude that marriage functioned to control sexuality. That is, it would appear that sexual intimacy was supposed to be confined to married couples and that societies would punish those who deviated from these expectations. However, Malinowski observed that there were plenty of other societies in which people did not value virginity prior to marriage or even held this status in contempt. Regardless of how much sexual freedom societies offered people, pregnancy was invariably a matter of concern, though. The objective of any society, he argued, was to prevent the birth of children whose paternity was not absolutely clear and socially established by the marriage of their mother and father.[4]

A concrete illustration of Malinowski's theory is provided by the analysis of Samoan courtship reported by Margaret Mead, a contemporary of Malinowski's. From her field interviews, she described adolescents in Samoa as freely engaging in premarital oral and manual sexual activities, but not in intercourse. Samoan norms allowed exceptions for teenaged boys when they consorted with older, postmenopausal women—because under these conditions intercourse could not be procreative. So fertile females did not risk condemnation as long as they avoided intercourse, and sexually active males lived up to social standards as long as they refrained from intercourse with these fertile females. Mead noted that, like people in most societies, the Samoans condemned promiscuous behavior. However, the point she was trying to make concerned what behavior the Samoans considered to be promiscuous. Her answer was that promiscuity meant engaging in intercourse that risked nonmarital reproduction.[5]

From analyzing premarital and extramarital patterns in many societies, Malinowski deduced that it was parenthood, not sexuality, that was universally tied to marriage. The reason for the tie, he ventured, was that if a woman with a child remained single, the child would be disadvantaged. Specifically, the child would lose the potential help of a father and of a father's kin, and a fatherless child's status in the community would be uncertain. Therefore, he claimed, as a family group, a woman and her offspring are sociologically both incomplete and illegitimate.

Malinowski's universal principle was revised and reformulated many times over the years, and it was utilized to explain norms and behaviors in many specific societies.[6] Its emphasis upon the link between marriage and parenthood remained the insightful core of the theory. However, to be of use to us as we examine both contemporary and historical societies, we will want to correct two of the biases that were built into most of the formulations. First, it was assumed that societies risked disintegration if they had more than a minimal number of out-of-wedlock births, and second, it was assumed that social institutions—rather than the individuals themselves—determined how individuals behaved. Although these two assumptions are interrelated, for convenience they can be discussed separately.

"Normal" Rates

Malinowski and his collaborators contended that whenever the rate of nonmarital births exceeded some very low value, it indicated that the society was in an abnormal, or pathological, state. Societies in this condition faced numerous adverse consequences because youngsters born without (social) fathers could not be properly socialized. As a result, they could not be counted on to perpetuate traditions. The strain on a society would ultimately become too great, and social disintegration could be expected soon to follow.

It is generally true that when out-of-wedlock rates increase, people in diverse societies contend that the increase presents a threat to their society, to public morality, and/or to the collective well-being. However, provinces of Austria in the mid-ninteenth century and many parts of the West Indies in the twentieth century have maintained nonmarital birth rates in excess of 50 percent for over a generation. In spite of the fears of contemporaries, Peter Laslett concludes, "social survival was apparently scarcely ever in question."[7] Thus, while high out-of-wedlock rates may cause strains, or be symptomatic of strains, they do not appear to be akin to societal or cultural genocide.

Institutions and Agents

Malinowski's initial presentation, as well as most of the sympathetic reformulations that came later, was cast in a functionalist mode that explained the consequences of various practices according to their presumed contributions to the maintenance of a society. In explaining marriage, socialization, or any other institutionalized actions, the functionalists emphasized what societies needed in order to maintain their major institutions intact. Thus marriage customs and rituals were explained functionally by the way they perpetuated the status of bride's and groom's families and by how they arranged kin according to the roles expected of them in the socialization of children. The imagery that girded these theories likened society to "an unseen hand" that regulated people so that their actions and their values were congruent with the needs of society, whether people realized it or not.

From this emphasis upon the coercive power of society, it followed, at least implicitly, that people were powerless automatons whose behavior was programmed to meet societal objectives. Many of these theories stressed how in the socialization process children came to internalize standards that guided their adult lives. The possibility that people, as adults, would deliberately act as their own agents was not pursued by the functionalists, who favored a view in which people were regarded as unreflectively following institutional scripts.[8]

It was women, in particular, who were not credited with much deliberation prior to acting. Thus if a society expected women to marry when they became pregnant, then the functionalist theories assumed that they would comply—without seriously evaluating how they might circumvent societal prescriptions in order to pursue "selfish" interests.[9] On the other hand, these same theories sometimes acknowledged the possibility that men had the discretion to intentionally set a course of action; for example, men might try to interpret marital rules in a way that would enable them to get out of marrying a pregnant girlfriend. (How successful their efforts would be, in the face of others' expectations, is a separate matter.)

Balancing Viewpoints

The balancing act we shall try to follow in this book is one that recognizes both men's and women's capacities for voluntary action, but does not exaggerate them to such a degree that people are thereby considered absolutely free to behave in whatever way they may happen to choose. It is hard to imagine a real society in which everyone shares the same values or an actual situation in which everyone's behavior precisely complies with a norm. Nevertheless, there is still some widespread agreement in societies concerning how people are supposed to act in a variety of circumstances and a reasonable degree of overt conformity with these shared expectations. Most women and men are more or less aware of these ideals and expectations and believe that they should comply with at least some of them, at least some of the time. Even when people might prefer not to comply, norms are still not irrelevant, because people cannot routinely violate norms with impunity, and they usually recognize this.[10] In addition, we do not relegate people to the status of automaton when we contend that norms and values have a way of insidiously influencing their thoughts and actions and tying them to the past, even in the face of social change.

Surrogate mothers provide an interesting and relevant illustration of the way that, despite extensive social changes, traditional institutional values continue to constrain behavior and affect people's thinking. For a fee, the surrogate carries the child of a man to whom she is not married, an arrangement that has become possible due to developments in modern obstetrics that would have been unimaginable in the past. Nevertheless, traditional conceptions of motherhood and of family life continue to shape the complex of role relationships that typically emerge around surrogacy. For example, recent research indicates that most surrogates try to forge a bond with the wife of the child's father rather than with the father. A visibly strong relationship between the surrogate and the wife can help to minimize even the appearance of adultery that otherwise might be evoked in such cases, given the fact that a woman other than a man's wife is carrying his child.

The powerful way that traditional values impact everyday life is also illustrated by the surrogates' descriptions of the meaning of their "work" in relation to conventional paid employment. A large percentage of them are working-class women who carry the fetus for a fee, but they have not usually been employed outside of their homes and do not generally favor women working for pay. So how do the surrogates reconcile their values with the payments they receive? As they describe their work and its meaning, they minimize the significance of the fee, stressing instead how their role enables them to give the "gift of life," making a nuclear family "whole" when spouses might otherwise be childless. Thus even as she works for pay, the surrogate's self-concept validates a very traditional view of motherhood as central to a woman's life.[11]

MARRIAGE AND LEGITIMACY

The view of parenthood presented by Malinowski and others did not rest upon either biological or moral considerations. It was the *social* role of a father that was stressed. As long as someone is recruited into this role and performs according to social expectations, then the child is not disadvantaged (or socially illegitimate), regardless of whether the social father is the biological father as well.

It would also be logically consistent with Malinowski's formulation to expect that children born to unmarried parents might later be "legitimized" by the subsequent marriage of their parents. This provision has, in fact, been part of the law of every European country since Roman times. The only limiting condition is that it must have been possible for the child's parents legally to have been married when the child was conceived. For example, neither could have been married to someone else at that time. Western church laws have mirrored secular laws in this respect, maintaining that marriage so powerfully sanctifies a relationship that even retroactively it can undo illegitimacy.[12]

If customs or laws specifying the ceremonial process by which a couple is to be married are reasonably clear in a society, then the wedlock status of any child would seem to be unambiguous. Only if the mother and father are married in the prescribed manner are their offspring considered legitimate. However, as is often the case with customs and laws, their applicability to individual cases can be uncertain, and when there is ambiguity, either formal or informal negotiation among the affected parties is typically required. In the contemporary United States, common-law marriages are particularly prone to a degree of uncertainty because they are based upon the parties' cohabitation and/or personal agreement. By definition, they involve no generally recognized religious or secular ceremonies one could point to as defining when a marriage occurred. By 1990, only thirteen states and the District of Columbia explicitly recognized these nonceremonial marriages, but many states other than those thirteen continued to enforce de facto common-law doctrine.

Several publicized common-law marriage disputes in recent years have involved celebrities. For example, the actor William Hurt was sued, in New York, by his former lover, who argued that they were legally married by common law in South Carolina as a result of living there together for a period of about one year while he was filming *The Big Chill*. In another publicized case, former baseball player Dave Winfield, a resident of New York at the time, was found by a jury in Houston, Texas, to be the common-law husband of a woman he had lived with between 1982 and 1985. Nearly five years after they separated, Winfield considered himself to be single and married another woman. However, the Houston jury held that he remained legally married to the first woman and hence could not legally marry the second.[13]

Celebrity palimony suits, such as Hurt's and Winfield's, periodically focus the public's attention on the potentially equivocal nature of a person's marital status. However, ambiguities are certainly neither confined to celebrities nor to the current United States. In Scotland during the late eighteenth century, for example, civil law recognized a couple as married if they had a wedding conducted in a church with the minister as the celebrant—or if there were any of the following: letters in which a man referred to a woman as his wife, witnesses who could testify that a woman was addressed as a man's wife in his presence and he did not contradict them, or promises of future marriage made by the man followed by sexual intercourse.

Any of these conditions, other than the church wedding, could be difficult to prove. The man and woman involved might have different recollections concerning whether promises had been made. Witnesses could disagree about who said what to whom, and when. And to complicate matters even further, the Scottish church did not accept all of these (secular) ways by which people ordinarily considered themselves to be married. Therefore, many couples could generally be recognized as legally married according to civil law, but not by church law.[14]

In most societies the marital status of most couples is usually clear-cut: they are or are not married according to relevant prescriptions. The status of their offspring is then unequivocal as well. In other cases, however, we have seen that the marital status of parents can be uncertain, and then the status of their children is in doubt too. As we examine diverse societies in later chapters of this book, we will need to be especially sensitive to the ways that changes in the prescribed religious or legal ceremonies in a society can suddenly validate or invalidate scores of marriages. Changes in which marriages are recognized would automatically result in dramatic increases or decreases in the official out-of-wedlock birthrate of that society. Thus if a class of marriages previously recognized as valid is, after the fact, no longer recognized, then offspring will—also after the fact—be reclassified from wedlock to out-of-wedlock.[15] These definition-induced changes in rates are of little interest to us because they are not accompanied by any corresponding changes in people's behavior.

To be more specific about the consequences of marriage, we should note that marriage is a necessary but not sufficient condition for legitimate offspring. The marriage of a child's mother obviously does not assure that her husband is the child's biological father or that he will be socially recognized as such. By way of background, let us acknowledge that most people never know for sure who fathered any particular child. (DNA testing is too limited and too recent to concern us as a qualification.) A woman who is sexually intimate with only one man may have no doubt about her child's paternity, but only she can know for sure, under most circumstances. When the woman has been intimate with men other than her husband, then even she may not be certain. Fatherhood must then be socially negotiated.

Because of the historically high rate of nonmarital sexual relations in Jamaica, the way fatherhood is determined in that Caribbean nation illustrates the processes that are typically involved, although more subtly, in establishing social fatherhood in most societies. Extensive premarital and extramarital relations have historically resulted in out-of-wedlock rates of 50 percent and higher in Jamaica. The true figure could be higher or lower than official estimates, however, depending upon how fatherhood is reckoned, and that is where negotiation processes fit into the picture.

Start with the case of a married woman who gives birth to a child and identifies her husband as the biological father. Does her husband believe that he is the father? Does the community? The child's status hangs in the balance as husband and community move toward closure. Their decision-making processes are highly interdependent: If the husband publicly accepts the child as his own, the community is likely to go along with him. On the other hand, if the community regards the child as his, the husband is more likely to be accepting. A key variable influencing the decision is the similarity in appearance of husband and child. Since Jamaica is multiracial, the similarity in husband's and child's skin color is especially relevant. If they share a strong resemblance, it will satisfy the community, and may also help a questioning husband to convince himself that he really is the biological father.

Any husband would usually like to be persuaded that he did father his wife's child, because that makes it easier for him to publicly accept the social role of father, and if he does, then the honor of everyone in the families involved, including his own honor, is protected. When people suspect that a Jamaican child's social and biological fathers are not the same, but the child is publicly presented as the offspring of the social father, the child is called a "jacket" in local gossip. The imagery implied is that a jacket child is something a husband "wears" to protect his honor. As one might expect in a society where a high rate of nonmarital births makes people suspicious, there is widespread teasing in Jamaica about children being jackets.[16]

Because there are more nonmarital conceptions in Jamaica than in the United States, paternity is more likely to involve problematic negotiations there than in the United States. However, the very same type of problem arises in the contemporary United States, if at a reduced scale. An interesting illustration is provided by the case of "Mr. G," a bus driver from Pittsburgh. For a half dozen years he lived with "Ms. X," though they never married. She bore two children during this period, a boy (in 1985) and a girl (in 1987). Shortly after the girl was born, they separated, but he signed a support order covering both children.

For the next six years he made monthly payments and regularly visited with both children. Then some relatives told him they heard gossip claiming another man fathered the little girl Mr. G was supporting. He confronted his former girlfriend and she admitted she had been seeing another man around the time the girl was conceived. A subsequent blood test confirmed that Mr. G was not the girl's father. He stopped making support payments for her and refused to have anything to do with her, though she was hurt by his sudden snub.

In family court the judge ruled that Mr. G had to resume the former support payments. The crucial consideration was the *initial* determination of fatherhood. Legally, it is almost impossible to change later. So "if a man thinks he is a father and acts like a father . . . that makes him a father even if he is unrelated to the child biologically," according to Pennsylvania state law—and that of most other states as well.[17]

In sum, it is not a child's actual paternity that is of interest to us here—after all, who knows?—but the way that the mother, her husband, and significant others in the community go about making that determination. This process of reckoning social fatherhood is always important in determining a child's status in the community.

LEGITIMACY AND INHERITANCE

One puzzling question that arises at this point is why pejorative terms, such as illegitimate or bastard, have historically been applied to the children of unmarried parents rather than to the parents. After all, any stigma to be assigned should appropriately be attributed to the parents, as individuals or as a couple, and not to the child. Individuals not married to each other that were believed to have engaged in sexual relationships have, in many societies, been publicly shamed for their actions: condemned as fornicators, branded with scarlet letters for adultery, and the like. However, these deviant labels were not primarily affixed to the woman, man, or both because a child resulted from the nonmarital intimacy, even though a visible pregnancy or the birth of a child may have been part of the evidence of adultery.

Some people might see this anomaly as an instance in which children are blamed for the sins of their parents, and I would be tempted to agree; but I do not think that contention provides the answer to the question of why demeaning labels have been affixed to the child that lacks a social father. One important part of the answer to this question lies in the rules governing the intergenerational transmission of property or, more specifically, in the *legitimacy* of any child's potential claim upon family wealth.

Questions concerning whether or not any specific child can inherit wealth obviously matter most to those families that possess sufficient wealth to transmit an unused portion of it to members of a succeeding generation. Therefore, we should not be surprised to learn that rules governing the conditions under which marriages will be recognized as producing legitimate offspring are most elaborate in societies where much wealth has been accumulated and that procedures for transmitting wealth are most explicit among the wealthiest, rather than poorest, segments within any society.[18]

The source of the connection among marriage, legitimacy, and inheritance is in ancient Greece. The Greeks had no word for family as we define it today. Most of their relevant writings were about the household (*oikos*), and the modern Greek word for family (*oikogenia*) combines the words for household and generation.[19] The household in ancient Greece was a coresidential unit, but most important, it was an ownership unit whose social meaning was equated with the totality of its possessions. The possessions of a household included both property and wealth and the people that were subject to the authority of the male head. The subordinated persons ordinarily included a wife and children, retainers, and slaves, and the total could include fifty persons or more in the most well-to-do Greek households.

The Romans continued the Greeks' emphasis upon households as property, and the difference between the classical and contemporary view of families can be gleaned from the kinds of censuses the Romans conducted. They took a detailed census of their empire every five years, counting the number of citizens and workers, and assessing taxes on land, animals, and wealth. However, the census takers never counted Roman household units. The obvious question is, Why not? According to Herlihy, it was because the several-hundred-person households of the Roman aristocrats were fundamentally different from, and could not be meaningfully compared to, the domestic units of the humble folks. As socially defined, the poor masses did not have households. Although men and women and their children lived together in residential units, these units were not thought of as households because they lacked sufficient wealth. Congruent with the view that the poorer strata did not have households, under early Roman law only the patricians, who comprised the dominant aristocracy, were permitted to marry. Literally defined, a patrician was a person who knew his father (*pater*) and who could inherit from him.[20]

Later Roman law clearly stated that the purpose of marriage was the procreation of children, and spelled out betrothal rituals, primarily consisting of an exchange of pledges of wealth and property from the families of the bride and groom. Marriages among everyone besides the extremely wealthy, from ordinary citizens to slaves, were either categorically prohibited or else seriously impeded by elaborate laws that prevented unions among persons who differed from each other in terms of social class, place of birth, and the like.

Through the Middle Ages in much of Europe, the small-household family attained greater legal significance, and both religious and secular rules prescribing how everyone was to be married were formulated. The control and transmission of wealth remained an integral feature of marriage ceremonies, and over the centuries, as societies amassed greater wealth, there were corresponding increases in the elaboration of marriage contracts. Thus in many modern nations, property law is incorporated into and is a major component of marriage law. In Sweden and other Nordic countries, for example, a significant portion of secular marriage legislation applies directly to the ownership and transmission of property, the preparation of wills, and various rules of inheritance.[21]

In sum, we note a close connection among marriage, parenthood, and inheritance. The legitimacy of a child is dependent upon his or her parents being "properly" married, and upon the assumption that the man in the role of his or her social father is also his or her biological father. While the terms illegitimate and bastard initially pertained specifically to a child's lack of inheritance rights, the application of these terms clearly became more diffuse and their meanings more pejorative, unfairly stigmatizing a child. In this book, therefore, we shall always rely upon more neutral descriptive terms, such as nonmarital or out-of-wedlock births, except in those few instances when the explicit referent is to inheritance rights.

DO FATHERS MATTER?

Surrounding the subject of out-of-wedlock births are questions about the limits of women's self-sufficiency as parents. It is, of course, technically possible for women to bear children without entering into any type of relationship with men.[22] Some would argue that as a result, our society has entered a new era in which marriage and procreation cannot continue to mean what they used to mean. For them, current concerns with out-of-wedlock births are mostly just another example of the turbulence that typically accompanies major social changes. It too will pass, and we will all adjust to a new set of realities.

The possible is not necessarily desirable, though, and there is a substantial amount of research that shows that fathers make a difference. (If one did not make that assumption, it would probably not make much sense to write about out-of-wedlock births!) To be specific, there are cross-cultural data that may indicate a fundamental bond between fathers and offsprings that is different from mothers' bonds, but nevertheless powerful. And this bond seems to play an important part in the development of both father and child.[23] In addition, a good deal of evidence can be marshalled to suggest that children raised without fathers are socially and emotionally deprived and that it is extremely difficult for a mother to compensate for a father's absence.[24]

Even if one assumes that fathers are somewhere between important and indispensable to their children, a variety of questions still remain unanswered. Specifically: Do parents have to be married for a man to be effective in the role of father? Can the father's role be played equally well by someone else—another woman, for example? How these questions are answered will impact how out-of-wedlock births are defined in the future, but these questions open up complex issues of contemporary marriage that are beyond the scope of this slim book. We will follow conventional definitions of both marriage and nonmarital childbearing, in the United States and elsewhere. We leave for others to explore questions about how marriage may be changing and the future implications of these changes for out-of-wedlock births.

NOTES

1. Associated Press, *Hartford Courant*, April 17, 1996, p. A4.

2. For a summary of the controversy, see "Dan Quayle vs. Murphy Brown," *Time*, June 1, 1992. For historical perspective on the character, see Mary A. Watson, "From 'My Little Margie' to 'Murphy Brown,' " *Television Quarterly*, 27, 2, 1994.

3. The preceding discussion of Ernestine Pallet is taken from Rachel G. Fuchs, *Poor and Pregnant in Paris* (New Brunswick, NJ: Rutgers University Press, 1992).

4. Bronislaw Malinowski, *Sex and Repression in Savage Society* (New York: Harcourt, Brace, 1927).

5. Nicole J. Grant, "From Margaret Mead's Field Notes: What Counted as 'Sex' in Samoa?" *American Anthropologist*, 97, Dec. 1995.

6. Among the most important reformulations were those advanced in essays by Kingsley Davis, "Illegitimacy and the Social Structure," *American Journal of Sociology*, 45, Sept. 1939, and William J. Goode, "A Deviant Case: Illegitimacy in the Caribbean," *American Sociological Review*, 25, Feb. 1960.

7. Peter Laslett, "Introduction," in Peter Laslett, Karla Oosterveen, and Richard M. Smith (Eds.), *Bastardy and Its Comparative History* (Cambridge, MA: Harvard University Press, 1980), p. 62. See also Robert B. Edgerton, *Sick Societies* (New York: Free Press, 1992).

8. For further discussion of the human-agency issue, see Paul Colomy and Gary Rhoades, "Toward a Micro Corrective of Structural Differentiation Theory," *Sociological Perspectives*, 37, Winter 1994.

9. See the critique of traditional family theory by Debra R. Kaufman, "Engendering Family Theory," in Jetse Sprey (Ed.), *Fashioning Family Theory* (Newbury Park, CA: Sage, 1990).

10. Durkheim is the sociological theorist who most clearly articulated this position. See especially chapter 1 in Emile Durkheim, *The Rules of the Sociological Method* (New York: Free Press, 1966; originally published in 1895).

11. Helena Ragoné, *Surrogate Motherhood* (Boulder, CO: Westview Press, 1994).

12. Jenny Teichman, *Illegitimacy* (Ithaca, NY: Cornell University Press, 1982).

13 For a review of both cases and others, see Ginny Carroll, "Marriage by Another Name," *Newsweek*, 114, July 24, 1989.

14. Rosalind Mitchison and Leah Leneman, *Sexuality and Social Control* (Oxford, UK: Basil Blackwell, 1989).

15. For an interesting discussion of how changes in social definitions caused dramatic increases in crime, heresy, and witch trials in Puritan Massachussetts, see Kai T. Erikson, *Wayward Puritans* (New York: Wiley, 1966).

16. Lisa Douglass, *The Power of Sentiment* (Boulder, CO: Westview Press, 1992).

17. *New York Times*, December 4, 1995, p. A18.

18. For a review of many relevant studies, see Gerhard E. Lenski, *Human Societies*, 7th ed. (New York: McGraw-Hill, 1995).

19. David Herlihy, *Medieval Households* (Cambridge, MA: Harvard University Press, 1985), pp. 2–5.

20. Ibid., pp. 2–3.

21. Teichman.

22. For a discussion of modern reproductive technology and the laws that regulate it, see Janet L. Dolgin, *Defining the Family* (New York: New York University Press, 1997).

23. See Wade C. Mackey, *The American Father* (New York: Plenum, 1996).

24. See the review by David Popenoe, *Life without Father* (New York: Free Press, 1996).

2

U.S. Data and Rates

Almost everyone realizes that there are a lot more single parents today, especially women, and that more of these contemporary women (and men) who are single parents have never been married. Impressions from everyday life support these conclusions, and they are regularly reinforced by media reports of the latest research. What is not so clear is how much the rate of unwed parenting increased over the years and whether the rate has actually begun recently to decline. Experts also disagree about how much teenagers or women who are nonwhite or less educated have contributed to the increase over the years. And there is the open question of the degree to which the United States has experienced a unique situation with respect to children born to unmarried parents.

In this chapter our first objectives are to examine the major sources that provide data pertaining to out-of-wedlock births and to assess the reliability of the various data sets. Then we will use the most accurate data available to describe in detail nonmarital birth patterns in American society, how they have changed over time, and how they compare to trends in other modern nations.

However, before we examine the data sources or immerse ourselves in the actual data, we will first introduce two women, Florence and Crystal, a mother and daughter from New York. We will review their experiences and then ask how the major data-collection enterprises would classify these two women and their out-of-wedlock children. Considering the alternatives will help us to understand the limitations in the data available. In addition, referring back to these women later as we present the data will help to give human faces to the statistics. This portrait of Florence and Crystal focuses upon their lives between 1984 and 1992, as described by Susan Sheehan, a Pulitzer Prize–winning author.[1]

FLORENCE AND CRYSTAL

In 1970, 17-year-old Florence Drummond of the Bronx had her first of five children. She named the baby girl Crystal. Over the next fourteen years she had four more children, fathered by different boyfriends, none of whom maintained lasting relationships with the children they fathered. All of the youngsters remained under Florence's care, but wound up shuttling back and forth from Florence to foster-care homes because she was unable to care for them continuously. For many years her cravings for heroin and cocaine kept her out on the streets day and night, and she often had no permanent address. She also served a week in jail in 1977 for welfare fraud.

In February of 1984, Florence had her last child. Eight months later, Crystal (Florence's eldest), now age 14 and living with her 23-year-old, drug-dealing boyfriend, gave birth to a son. Despite having a child, Crystal was legally a child herself. Being unable to care for her son and not having a responsible parent to care for her, Crystal did not have much choice but agree to separate foster-care accommodations for her son and herself. In 1985, St. Christopher's, a Catholic agency in New York, placed her son in the home of a New York family, and she was assigned to a neighborhood group home that housed six young women in three bedrooms. The agency provided room and board and around the clock custodial supervision of Crystal and the other residents.

Crystal spent several years in the group home, experiencing a difficult adolescence: she was in and out of school, frequently in trouble for violating house or school rules. Finally, she was out on her own. In 1989 Crystal was working full-time in the mailroom of a New York firm and had her own apartment. Her son, Daquan, now 5 years old, remained in foster care primarily because, as Crystal put it, she had little patience with being a parent. However, she was spending a great deal of time in her mother's apartment and doing things with her mother and her younger siblings, who were now reunited with their mother.

Florence and her younger children were, in 1989, living on welfare, that is, AFDC, which provided her with $313 per month plus $271 per month in food stamps. However, Florence's life on the dole hit a snag when the public assistance office in New York discovered that she still owed money from her earlier welfare fraud in 1977. To gain recompense, New York reduced her stipend, and she found herself unable to pay the monthly rent on her apartment. Crystal, at the same time, was struggling to pay off some big bills she had accumulated for clothing and to replace her television set, which had been stolen in a robbery.

Mother and daughter were confronting these economic problems when they were recruited by a "broker" to marry illegal aliens who needed U.S. citizens as spouses in order to remain in the United States. Each of the illegal residents, originally from Morocco, Nigeria, and elsewhere, was willing to pay as much as $1,500 to a woman who would marry him and then help him to convince the Immigration and Naturalization Service that theirs was a bona fide marriage. Both Florence and Crystal took the money and played their parts.

Through the time Florence was in her early forties and Crystal was in her middle twenties, these marriages-for-profit were the only formal marriages into which either of them entered. The financial arrangement did not work out well for Florence, though. A few months later officials threatened her with the loss of food-stamp benefits when they discovered that she was legally married. So she wound up paying more to obtain a divorce from the Moroccan than the broker originally paid her to marry him.

By early in 1992, Florence's drug dependency was sufficiently under control that she was able to obtain a full-time job, and with the help of food stamps, she was able to make ends meet without AFDC. Her younger children lived in her apartment most of the time, but they were regularly in trouble for fighting or stealing, and she periodically found them so unruly that she shuffled them off to foster homes.[2] In the summer of 1992, Crystal took her then 7-year-old son out of foster care and found a small, one-bedroom apartment four blocks from Florence's. In the fall of 1992, their children began playing and going to school together, and Crystal's son regularly slept over at his grandmother's apartment (whether or not Crystal's boyfriend happened to be sleeping in his home that night).

We can hope that Florence's and Crystal's circumstances (and those of their children) continued to improve, but this is where our knowledge of their lives ends. In any event, though, it would be difficult to justify devoting more space to them, because it is obvious that no one or two women, such as Florence and Crystal, could possibly be totally representative of the thousands of women who each year have children outside of marriage. However, as we will see in the tables and figures to be presented in this chapter, they do personify many of the statistical attributes most typical of single mothers.

DATA SOURCES

The popular media regularly announce statistics pertaining to out-of-wedlock birthrates in both the nation and local areas. The issue is of such contemporary significance that when updated figures are released by a government agency or private poll, they frequently provide one of the lead stories on evening newscasts. Did you ever wonder how the figures are obtained, or how accurate they are?

The best estimates of nonmarital birthrates and ratios in the United States are gleaned from three distinct data sources: (1) the Bureau of the Census publications, which enumerate relationships among persons living in the same households; (2) the National Center for Health Statistics, whose Vital Statistics tabulates information provided on birth certificates; and (3) longitudinal surveys, which track the experiences and attitudes of samples of the same people over various time intervals. Although all three sources yield very useful information and provide distinctive insights into out-of-wedlock births, each typically has limitations as well. Therefore, we will pay close attention to the ways in which the reliability of each data source can be compromised.

The Census

Major sources of pertinent information are the population analyses of the U.S. Bureau of the Census. Neither the complete Census of Population taken once each decade nor the special studies periodically published between decades specifically tabulate nonmarital or out-of-wedlock births, but they do compile figures on marriage and divorce, fertility, household and living arrangements, and so on. Of particular relevance are the bureau's detailed enumerations of the adults and children living in all U.S. households, and the (reported) relationships among all of them. Errors creep into census figures because they rely upon people's knowledge and honesty, and either may be limited, but errors in people's self-reports are not a major problem in census publications. A more serious limitation of the Census of Population is that despite its mission to provide a complete enumeration of the United States, it has always been incomplete. Households in inner-city, minority neighborhoods are notably underincluded, and because nonmarital birthrates have been especially high in these communities, inferences from census figures may underestimate the true number of children born out of wedlock.[3] Nevertheless, each decade's census does provide the most exhaustive and complete data for the U.S. population at the precise point in time at which it is conducted. In addition, the Census Bureau updates many parts of the census every two years with a *Current Population Report*, based upon information provided by a representative sample of the population.

The core figures in Census of Population documents dichotomize women according to whether they ever married and then divide those who have according to whether their husbands are present in the household. It is reasonably easy to tabulate some out-of-wedlock statistics by counting the households that are comprised of women who have never married and their children. These figures provide the census data's most uncompromised indicators of out-of-wedlock rates, and we will focus upon never-married mothers in several of the tables that follow.

There is little uncertainty concerning how to interpret households identified in the census as those comprised of a married woman, a husband who is present, and children. Most analysts regard any children in such households as in-wedlock, or marital, births even though the census figures do not disclose whether the husband who is present is also the biological or adopted father. The households most difficult to classify are those comprised of children and a woman who has married, but whose husband is not present due to death, separation, or divorce. Because the census data do not inform the reader of *when* the husband departed, such households are especially ambiguous with respect to out-of-wedlock births.

It may be helpful here again to examine the type of assumptions made about census data in relation to Florence and Crystal, two cases for which we have a good deal of additional information. First, with respect to Florence, her brokered marriage occurred well after all of her children were born. Using any census enumeration conducted prior to her short-lived marriage would have correctly classified her household as containing five children born out of wedlock. Given a snapshot of her household after her status changed to married and then divorced, we would probably find ourselves unable to make assumptions about the father, or fathers, of Florence's children.[4]

With respect to Crystal's household as it would be described in census tables, prior to her marriage her son would have been correctly classified as an out-of-wedlock birth. However, if Crystal remained married to, but physically separated from, the former illegal alien from Nigeria, we would be unsure what to assume about her son or any subsequent children she might have. We happen to know it would be very unlikely for her legal husband to be the father of any such children, due to the fact that he and she had absolutely no relationship, but we would not know this if we had only census data at our disposal.

In sum, as we make inferences from census tabulations, we will usually equate out-of-wedlock births with births to never-married women. The classification that results will not contain any errors, that is, it will not include in the out-of-wedlock category any births that should not be considered out of wedlock. The disadvantage to relying upon births to never-married women is that their total does not contain all out-of-wedlock births, hence it understates the true ratio of out-of-wedlock to all births. Any other classification strategy would inflate estimates of out-of-wedlock births with errors of unknown size. The conservativeness of this approach recommends it, especially because supplementary survey data enable us to estimate that around three-fourths of all nonmarital births in the United States have, in recent years, occurred to never-married women. For example, of all the women who had a nonmarital birth in the five years preceding a 1987–88 survey, 61 percent occurred to women who had never married at the time of delivery and who had still never married at the time of the survey. An additional 16 percent had never married at the time they gave birth but had married by the time of the interview. Thus, never-married women comprised just over three-quarters of all of the women who had a nonmarital birth. (The status of the other unmarried mothers was either widowed, separated, or divorced.)[5]

Vital Statistics

The bottom section of the Standard Certificate of Live Birth asks the following question:

MOTHER MARRIED? (At birth, conception, or any time between)   (Yes or no)

This question is typically answered by the mother. Whoever attends the birth (usually a physician, sometimes a midwife or other aid provider) signs the top part of the certificate to attest that a live birth has occurred, but no one is responsible for verifying the marital status reported by the mother or for corroborating other personal characteristics she reports. If, for example, a woman erroneously believes that her cohabiting boyfriend (and father of her child) is legally considered her husband, she may unwittingly give false information. She may intentionally lie on the birth certificate and claim she is married when she is not because she is embarrassed to acknowledge her status to anyone, or she may falsely deny the existence of her husband because she is afraid the truth will adversely affect her eligibility to receive welfare benefits.

Perhaps by interrogating at length each woman who delivers a child, it might be possible to ascertain which of them is telling the truth. Collecting data in this manner would obviously be very expensive, though, and such efforts are hardly warranted. For research purposes, the most practical way to assess the probable truthfulness of people's replies to any question (on a birth certificate, for example) is to ask them the same question on a different document and then compare their answers. Researchers assume that consistency in a respondent's answers is a prerequisite for truthfulness, so when people are not consistent, a lack of candor is indicated. The same logic is followed by parents who insist that children retell how they happened to get in trouble at school, and then pounce upon discrepancies in the story. The underlying inferential principle is that if, at roughly the same time, people give different replies to the same question, they are probably hiding something or trying to be evasive. People who give consistent answers to the same question at least *may* be giving truthful replies.

Assessments of self-reported marital status on birth certificates show a high consistency of response. For example, a national sample of women who recently gave birth were asked their marital status as part of a survey of infant health. Their answers were subsequently compared to the marital status information they provided on the infant's birth certificate. Overall consistency was about 95 percent,[6] which compares very favorably to the degree of agreement found among people's answers to any type of question. Thus replies to the marital-status question on birth certificates appear to provide reliable information. From a research standpoint, that makes it especially regrettable that all states' birth certificates do not ask the mother's marital status. The question is asked in the standard U.S. form, but states are not required to use it, and several of the largest states (including New York and California) have not. The forms in use in most of these other states do not ask the mother's marital status. In all, at least as late as 1993, about one-third of the U.S. population resided in states that did not ask the mother's marital status.

In some states that did not employ the standard birth certificate, the forms in use did ask the surnames of mother and father, and analysts have used this as the best information then available to gauge out-of-wedlock births. Researchers specifically assumed that if the surnames of mother and father were different from each other, then the birth was nonmarital. However, following this procedure can inflate calculations of the nonmarital birthrate by incorrectly including as nonmarital the births to married women who retained their maiden names. What would make this especially hazardous to analyses is that the percentage of married women keeping their maiden names has increased since the middle of the twentieth century. Therefore, relying upon a comparison of surnames, by itself, would falsely magnify estimates of how much out-of-wedlock births had increased.[7]

In addition, relying on given surnames to infer out-of-wedlock births can introduce other errors of unknown magnitude. To illustrate, consider Crystal's dilemma when her son, Daquan, was born. New York was one of the states whose birth certificates did not ask marital status, but did ask mother's and father's surnames. Little Daquan's father was Daquan Jefferson, and Crystal never hesitated in entering Jefferson on the line that asked for father's surname. Filling in mother's (i.e., her own) surname required some reflection, though. Crystal had, in the past, ordinarily gone by her father's surname, Taylor, and she considered that possibility now; but she also regarded herself as a part of big Daquan's family (calling his mother "Ma") so Jefferson was another alternative. Finally, because her hospital stay was going to be paid for by her mother's Medicaid, Crystal decided to enter Florence's surname, Drummond.

It was hit-and-miss as to whether the parents' surnames provided by Crystal on little Daquan's birth certificate would later enable an analyst to accurately classify her son's birth as out-of-wedlock, though Crystal's final surname report was not misleading on this score. Limiting even further the use of surname analysis, some states that do not employ the standard birth certificate do not permit any information about the father, including his surname, to be included on their state form if the mother is not married. Therefore, it is fortunate (for research purposes, at least) that about two-thirds of all births occur in states where marital status is asked on the standard certificate—and, as we have seen, that it appears to be answered truthfully.

Longitudinal Surveys

The final data source we will employ to describe the contemporary United States consists of a number of longitudinal surveys. These surveys track large samples of people, and young people in particular, periodically monitoring their dating and sexual experiences, use of contraceptives, cohabitation, and so forth. Most of the surveys we will discuss were not primarily designed to provide information about out-of-wedlock births, but the data they contain are often quite relevant.

The distinct advantage of these surveys arises from the fact that they follow the same people over time, reinterviewing them in "waves." Therefore, unlike census or vital statistics data, which provide static pictures of people at one point in time, these surveys illuminate the sequences of events in people's lives. These data are unique in the way they can be used to illuminate such questions as when a woman's birth and divorce occurred in relation to each other or the chronology of events leading to marriage, birth, household formation, and so forth.

Two of the surveys whose findings we shall refer to in the following pages are illustrative of the genre. First is the National Survey of Families and Households, which interviewed 13,000 respondents in 1987–88 and reinterviewed 10,000 of the original sample in 1992–94.[8] Data from the 1987–88 wave of that survey provided our estimate of the percentage of all out-of-wedlock births that occur to never-married women. Our second example is the National Longitudinal Survey of Youth, which began in 1978–79 with a sample of about 15,000 young people. They have been repeatedly questioned in the ensuing years regarding their attitudes and participation in familial, religious, and sexual activities and in school and work.[9]

Partially detracting from the value of most longitudinal surveys is a problem with attrition: the tendency for respondents to drop out over time. If the losses are selective, attrition can bias the later waves in a sample. Some of the people in any initial sample move and leave no forwarding address; others refuse to be interviewed again; some die before they can be recontacted. The resulting attrition can leave holes in the subsamples that remain, thereby limiting the generalizability of the data. For example, when the National Longitudinal Survey of Youth began, it contained a large number of white females and small, but adequate, subsamples of black and Hispanic females. By later waves, however, each of the latter two subsamples became so small that some analyses had to be confined to white females.

In sum, there are no perfect data in the real world, so we will be on the firmest ground when we rely upon data from many sources, so that their limitations are offsetting. Fortunately, as we will later note, there is found reasonable consistency among many census, Vital Statistics, and longitudinal survey figures, which buoys our confidence in all of them. It is important, however, continuously to regard all the figures presented as approximate rather than precise measures.

NONMARITAL RATES

The best-known and most widely cited statistic for describing non-marital births in a society is the out-of-wedlock (or nonmarital) birth-*rate*. It is a measure of the proportion of unmarried women, aged 15 to 44, who give birth to a child in any given year. To calculate the rate, one divides the number of nonmarital births by the number of unmarried women (and by convention, multiplies that figure by 1,000). By contrast, the *ratio*, discussed in the following section, indicates the proportion of all births to unmarried mothers. Neither statistic is intrinsically better than the other. The choice of which to use rests upon whether one wants to know about the fertility behavior of unmarried women (the rate) or the status of infants' mothers (the ratio).[10] It is unfortunate that the two sound alike, because they can differ from each other, and it leads to confusion when one is mistaken for the other.

Let us begin with a long-term view, employing vital statistic data (i.e., data from birth certificates). Over slightly more than one-half century, between 1940 and 1995, there was a dramatic increase in this rate, as shown in figure 2.1.

In 1940, fewer than 10 in 1,000—less than 1 in 100—unmarried women had a child. By the early 1950s, the rate doubled, but was still very low by contemporary standards. The rate continued to increase rapidly until 1970, when both marital and nonmarital fertility declined. Near the end of that decade, the rate again began to increase, and its incline was very steep during the 1980s, until the rate flattened in the early 1990s. Then Vital Statistics figures for 1995 stated that for every 1,000 unmarried women, there were 44.9 live births, almost 2 percentage points lower than in 1994. Most of the media hyped this reported finding and claimed that a troubling social problem was ebbing. Much too much was made of the decline, however, for several reasons that bear explanation.

Figure 2.1
Nonmarital Rates, 1940–1995 (Births per 1,000 Unmarried Women)

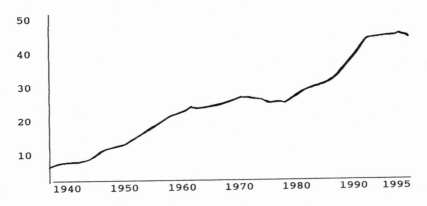

First, about one-half of the 1994–95 decline was more apparent than real, due to a change in reporting practices in the state of California. Recall from the discussion of vital statistics that California had been one of the states that inferred marital status from a comparison of surnames on babies' birth certificates. In 1995 the state changed its procedure, and like most of the rest of the nation, directly asked the mother's marital status. This new mode of calculating nonmarital births in the state, first reported for 1995, almost certainly increased the accuracy of California's tally. However, it resulted in a large drop in the state's nonmarital birthrates, previously inflated by dubious inferences about mother's marital status. The decline in California's rate should, of course, be regarded as a statistical correction rather than a genuine change. When the effect of that state's new reporting procedure is taken into account, the rate for the entire country still declined, but by less than 1 percentage point.

Second, the nonmarital birthrate had increased between 1993 and 1994 from 45.3 per 1,000 women to 46.9. A comparison of 1995 to 1993, net of California's statistical correction in 1995, indicates that the rate was higher in 1995 than in 1993. So no meaningful downward trend is indicated. Furthermore, given that between 1991 and 1993 the nonmarital birthrate was virtually unchanged, the conclusion that seems most reasonable is that through the first half of the 1990s the nonmarital birthrate—as indicated by birth-certificate records—was essentially unchanged.

We can take another look at recent changes in the nonmarital birth rate from another vantage point by employing data from the Census Bureau's *Current Population Reports*. These figures, it will be recalled, are gathered every other year from specially selected samples of households.· Respondents in these households report upon their marital status and whether they had a birth in the past year. Unlike the data compiled from birth certificates, no recent changes in procedures could be responsible for extrinsic fluctuations in the census data. Unfortunately, as this book is written, they do not provide any information about fertility after June 1994, but they can provide a very focused view until then.

For this assessment we will only examine never-married women. There can be some ambiguity, we have noted, in the unmarried category of the census's classification. The most error-free category is the never-married mothers (which we know will include about three-quarters of all unmarried women who have a child). From 1992 to 1994, the proportion of never-married women who had a child in the preceding year increased, whether the target variable is first births (from 17.3 to 22.5 per 1,000) or total births (from 35.1 to 39.2 per 1,000).[11]

In sum, figures from household surveys reported by the Census Bureau translate into higher estimated rates of nonmarital childbearing than figures from Vital Statistics' analysis of birth certificates. The census figures also indicate continued increases in nonmarital birthrates into the 1990s, though the pace of the increase slackened. It will probably be some years before this issue is completely resolved. Both the Census Bureau and Vital Statistics reported sizable increases in 1994 from either 1992 or 1993. Was that increase an anomaly, justifying the conclusion that rates flattened? Alternatively, was the decline reported for 1995 the anomaly, a correction perhaps for the larger increase in 1994, and merely a temporary halt to the long-term upward trend? Figures for the rest of the 1990s may be necessary before these questions can be answered. Until then, the safest conclusion is probably that nonmarital birthrates increased a small amount during the first half of the 1990s.

Subgroup Differences

The rates we have presented so far are summaries for the entire (at-risk) population. While they are instructive, the figures lose some of their meaning when subgroups within the population are very different from each other. By analogy, no one took the old statistician seriously when, standing with one foot in a bucket of ice and the other in a bucket

of steaming hot water, he proclaimed that on average he was comfort-
able! What detracts from the averages we have been presenting is the
fact that when we examine nonmarital fertility by age, education, and
race-ethnicity, we see subgroups almost as different from each other as
the water temperature in the old statistician's buckets.

Race-Ethnicity

To begin, we look at first births before first marriages for women in
the three major racial-ethnic groups at the start of each of the last four
decades. These census figures are displayed in figure 2.2.[12]

From figure 2.2 we can see that first births before first marriages became increasingly common among women in all three racial groups over
the past thirty-five years. However, black women began the period at a
much higher rate, and the three groups maintained their relative rank-
ing—blacks highest, Hispanics second, whites third—throughout the

Figure 2.2
First Births before First Marriage

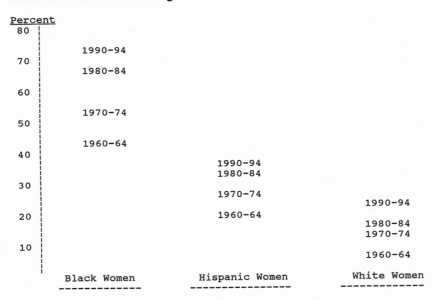

Source: Adapted from Terry Lugaila, *Households, Families, and Children,* U.S. Bureau of
the Census, Current Population Reports, Series P23–181 (Washington, DC: GPO, 1992).
The 1990–94 estimated have been adjusted with figures from Amara Bachu, *Fertility
of American Women: June 1994,* Current Population Reports, Series P20–482
(Washington, DC: GPO, 1995).

period. Further, despite some sizable absolute and percentage increases in out-of-wedlock birthrates among both white and Hispanic women, their rates in the 1990s remained below those of black women in the 1960s.

To understand some of the increases in more human terms, let us again consider Florence and Crystal. When Florence gave birth to Crystal in 1970, slightly over one-half of all first births to African American women involved mothers who, like Florence, had never married. By the time Crystal gave birth to her son in 1984, over two-thirds of all black mothers having their first child were, like Crystal, never married. By the mid-1990s, the rate of unmarried childbearing among new black mothers reached over three-quarters.

While white women entered the 1960s with few first births before first marriages, their rate of increase (partly because they began from such a low figure) has been very high. Between 1992 and 1994, for example, the nonmarital birthrate among blacks did not continue to increase, but it did among white women. In the recent past, a number of trends relating to sexual activity and marriage began first among blacks, with whites following later. Out-of-wedlock rates seem likely to provide another example of this pattern, and we will note still others. This pattern has led columnist William Rasberry to comment that "if you want to see how black problems would look wearing a white face, just wait a generation."[13]

Educational Level

Historically there have been marked variations in nonmarital birthrates among women in different educational levels, and the contrasts continue to be about as pronounced as those among racial-ethnic groups. Simply put, the higher the level of education, the lower the rate. For example, the population survey of the census report for women who had a baby in the year ending June 1994 is summarized in table 2.1.

The high rate of nonmarital births among females who did not complete high school is difficult to interpret from census figures because of uncertainty about the ordering of events. Are girls who become pregnant in high school—almost all of whom are unmarried—more likely to drop out? Or is it that girls who drop out are more likely to become pregnant? Neither Vital Statistics nor Census Bureau data are very useful in trying to answer these questions, because both are cross-sectional. That is, they provide data on the population at one point in time, which is more akin to a photograph than to a motion picture. In order to clarify

Table 2.1
Women Who Had a Baby in the Year Ending June 1994

Educational Level Completed	% Not Married
Less than High Scool	46
High School Graduate	30
Some College	17
Bechelor's Degree (or more)	6

Source: Amara Bachu, *Fertility of American Women: June 1994,* Current Population Reports, Series P20-482 (Washington, DC: GPO, 1995), table 4.

how a sequence of events occurs, longitudinal surveys (which track a specially selected sample of people across time) are indispensable.

Particularly pertinent figures from the National Educational Longitudinal Study focus upon those females who had a child within four years of the time they completed eighth grade, in other words, at high-school age. In total, 62 percent of the girls who bore a child out of wedlock dropped out of school at some point. Because the investigators followed these girls over time, they knew that one-fourth dropped out *before* they became pregnant, "suggesting they were already disengaging from school."[14] About 37 percent dropped out after they became pregnant, some because of their condition, but for others it was only the last straw in their premature departure from high school.

Age

Recent increases in nonmarital births can be traced to an increase that began among teenagers around 1970. Between 1970 and 1975, births per 1,000 women declined in every age group—except among teenagers, where they increased. Then between 1975 and 1980, out-of-wedlock rates for all women 29 and under increased, while staying the same among women 30 and over. Thus, prior to the "epidemic-like" increases of the 1980s, nonmarital birth rate increases were clearly age linked. In the 1980s, and especially between 1985 and 1990, however, rates went up substantially across the age spectrum. Then during the first half of the 1990s, the rate with which nonmarital births increased slowed in every age group, but least so among teenagers and women aged 24 and under.[15]

In 1994, women aged 20–24 had the highest rate of nonmarital births and contributed 35 percent of the total. Women 25–29 had the second highest rate but contributed only 18 percent of all out-of-wedlock births, and teenagers had the third highest rate of any age group but contributed 31 percent of such births. The discrepencies between relative rates and contributions to the total are due to differences in the size of the age cohorts. At no time in the past forty years have teenagers had a higher nonmarital birthrate than women in their twenties. When circa 1990 there were more nonmarital births to teens than to any other age group, it was, in large measure, because teens comprised a very large proportion of the childbearing population.

Some writers heralded the declining percentage of all nonmarital births contributed by teenagers as evidence that the public had overreacted to the problem of teenage pregnancy.[16] Several disquieting trends persist, though. First, the teen out-of-wedlock rate dropped during the 1990s primarily as a result of declines among older teens, aged 18 and 19. The birthrate among girls aged 17 and under continued to increase, and almost all of these births were out of wedlock.[17] And it is these youngest single mothers who are most unable to properly care for their children. Finally, the decline in the proportion of nonmarital births contributed by teenagers should not be a source of solace because, as we have noted, that decline was largely due to relative shrinkage of the teen cohort. Census Bureau projections show that by the year 2000, the number of teenagers will again increase, and become the largest age cohort among women of childbearing ages.[18] Therefore, unless marital and birth patterns change among teenagers, they will, in short time, again be the largest contributors to out-of-wedlock births.

NONMARITAL RATIOS

Next we turn to an examination of the nonmarital birth ratio, that is, the proportion of all births that are out of wedlock. Unlike the rate, which examines women's fertility, the ratio focuses upon the proportion of infants born to unmarried parents. The long-term trend in the out-of-wedlock ratio is presented in figure 2.3.

In contrast to the rate, the ratio followed a steadier upward spiral across the half century, and its increase, in percentage terms, was even more dramatic: from less than 4 percent of all births in 1940 to nearly 34 percent of all births in 1994. Part of this large increase, as we previously noted, was due to the simultaneous decline in the marital fertility rate.

Figure 2.3
Nonmarital Ratios, 1940–1995 (Proportion of Births to Unmarried Women)

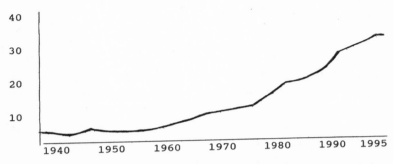

Source: Primarily adapted from Stephanie J. Ventura, Christine A. Bachrach, Laura Hill, Kelleen Kaye, Pamela Holcomb, and Elisa Koff, "The Demography of Out-of-Wedlock Childbearing," in U.S. Department of Health and Human Services, *Report to Congress on Out-of-Wedlock Childbearing* (Hyattsville, MD, 1995), p.7; and supplemented with information from H. M. Rosenberg, "Births and Deaths: United States, 1995," *Monthly Vital Statistics Report,* Vol. 45, Supp. 2, 1996

Like the rate, a decline in the ratio (to 32 percent) was reported for 1995, but here again much of the small apparent decline was due to California's changed reporting procedures. The most plausible conclusion is that the nonmarital birth ratio *may* have stabilized in the mid-1990s.

The out-of-wedlock ratio is an example of an "incidence" statistic. It pertains to the number of new cases—nonmarital births in a year—and not the total number of such children that exist. However, one important reason for differentiating the out-of-wedlock ratio from the rate is to be able to focus in upon how many children begin life with an unmarried parent. It is of some relevance, then, also to examine the "prevalence" measure, that is, to note how the proportion of all children living with an unmarried parent has increased. In 1970, only 12 percent of American children under age 18 lived with one parent. By 1994, this figure more than doubled, to 27 percent. Further, and of even more relevance to us, in 1970 the single parent with a child under age 18 was nearly five times more likely to be divorced than never married, but divorced and never-married were equally likely among single parents by 1994.[19]

We will not repeat the description of subgroup differences here. We will simply note that, as would be expected, out-of-wedlock children are characterized by the same racial and ethnic distributions as their mothers.

CONTEMPORARY COMPARISONS

To complete our overview of out-of-wedlock rates in the United States, we turn to a brief comparison of industrial nations. It will be kept brief here because later chapters of this book provide extensive comparative data. National differences in how the relevant information is recorded make it difficult to be exact in these comparisons, and differences in the age distributions of their populations (compositional effects, as previously described) can distort comparisons among nations. Nevertheless, we may note that rates in the contemporary United States appear to be in the middle range relative to the other industrial nations. Figures for a sample of nations, in 1992, are presented in table 2.2.

With only a few exceptions among industrial nations, out-of-wedlock birthrates have been increasing during the past thirty to forty years or so. Both timing and composition have varied, though. Most resembling the United States overall is the United Kingdom. Rates in both countries increased from roughly midcentury to about 1970, more or less flattened for the better part of a decade, and then increased rapidly in the 1980s.[20] Most distinctive about the U.S. increase, however, has been the extremely high rate of out-of-wedlock births to teenagers, especially

Table 2.2
Percentage of Births to Unmarried Women

Country	%
Sweden	50
Denmark	48
United Kingdom	31
France	31
United States	30
Canada (est.)	28
Germany	15
Italy	7
Japan	1

Source: Adapted from Stephanie J. Ventura, Christine A. Bachrach, Laura Hill, Kellen Kaye, Pamela Holcomb, and Elisa Koff, "The Demography of Out-of-Wedlock Childbearing," in U.S. Department of Health and Human Services, *Report to Congress on Out-of-Wedlock Childbearing* (Hyattsville, MD, 1995), figure VII-1.

black teenagers. In other English-speaking nations, such as Canada, England, and Wales, by contrast, the greatest increases occurred among women in their late twenties, and in still other nations, such as Australia, the largest increases have occurred among women in their thirties.[21] There is some evidence that recent age patterns within the United States are becoming more like those of other English-speaking nations, as the contribution of teen births to out-of-wedlock rates has declined somewhat.

In the chapters that follow, we will present out-of-wedlock data pertaining to a number of different nations. In chapter 7 we will return to a more detailed examination of the place of the United States in a contemporary international perspective.

NOTES

1. The description of Florence and Crystal is taken from Susan Sheehan, *Life for Me Ain't Been No Crystal Stair* (New York: Pantheon Books, 1993).

2. Temporary or permanent foster care has become increasingly common, especially for African American children. Just in the years 1986 to 1993, the foster-care population increased from about 290,000 children nationally to 450,000. African American children were more likely than white children ever to be placed in foster care, and once placed, they left at slower rates and had higher rates of reentry. As a result of all these differences, in 1993 African American children were about six times more likely than whites to be in foster care at any particular time. For additional information, see U.S. General Accounting Office, *Child Welfare*, GAO/HEHS-95–208 (Washington, DC: Government Printing Office [GPO], September 1995).

3. For a discussion of problems with the 1990 census, see Steven A. Holmes, "Census Officials Plan Big Changes in Gathering Data," *New York Times*, May 16, 1994, p. A1. See also David W. Stewart and Michael A. Kamins, *Secondary Research* (Thousand Oaks, CA: Sage Publications, 1993).

4. We are focusing exclusively upon the mother's children in this discussion, but it should be recognized that similar misclassifications could occur with children brought by their father to a recombined or reconstituted family.

5. Data from this survey and others are summarized in Kristin A. Moore, "Nonmarital Childbearing in the United States," in U.S. Department of Health and Human Services, *Report to Congress on Out-of-Wedlock Childbearing* (Hyattsville, MD, 1995), p. viii.

6. Kenneth C. Schoendorf, Jennifer D. Parker, Leonid Z. Batkhan, and John L. Kiely, "Comparability of Birth Certificate and 1988 Maternal and Infant Health Survey," *Vital and Health Statistics*, Series 2, No. 116 (Washington, DC: National Center for Health Statistics, 1993).

7. For further discussion of birth certificates and the quality of the data produced by them, see Section 4, Technical Appendix, in National Center for Health Statistics, *Vital Statistics of the United States, 1991*, Vol. 1, Natality (Washington, DC: Public Health Service, 1995).

8. For further description, see Appendix A in Larry Bumpass, "The Declining Significance of Marriage," NSFH Working Paper #66 (Madison, WI: University of Wisconsin, 1994).

9. For further information, see Center for Human Resource Research, *NLS Handbook 1991* (Columbus, OH: Ohio State University, 1991).

10. For further discussion, see Herbert L. Smith and Phillips Cutright, "Thinking about Change in Illegitimacy Ratios," *Demography*, 25, 1988; see also Pritwis Das Gupta, *Standardization and Decomposition of Rates*. U.S. Bureau of the Census, Current Population Reports, P23–186. (Washington, DC: GPO, 1993).

11. These figures are from Amara Bachu, *Fertility of American Women: June 1992*, Current Population Reports, P20–470 (Washington, DC: GPO, 1993); and Amara Bachu, *Fertility of American Women: June 1994*, Current Population Reports, P20–482 (Washington, DC: GPO, 1995).

12. This figure has been adjusted for all women of childbearing ages.

13. William Rasberry, "Vanishing Families, Disposable Men," *Washington Post National Weekly Edition*, April 8–14, 1996, p. 26.

14. Quote and figures from Kristin A. Moore, *Facts at a Glance* (Washington, DC: Child Trends, 1996), p. 2.

15. See U.S. Department of Health and Human Services, *Report to Congress*, and Rosenberg.

16. See, for example, Kristin Luker, *The Politics of Teenage Pregnancy* (Cambridge, MA: Harvard University Press, 1996).

17. See Moore. p. 1

18. See Bachu, 1995, p. 4.

19. Figures from Arlene F. Saluter, *Marital Status and Living Arrangements: March 1994*, U.S. Bureau of the Census, Current Population Reports, Series P20–484 (Washington, DC: GPO, 1996), table E.

20. Ibid., Figures VII–2 and 3; see also Phillips Cutright and Herbert L. Smith, "Trends in Illegitimacy among Five English-Speaking Populations," *Demography*, 23, 1986.

21. Ibid. We will explore the specific components of the increase in the United States in substantial detail in the chapter that immediately follows this one, then examine a diverse historical and international sample in the two chapters that follow.

3

Nonmarital Births: Who, How, and When

The rate with which all sorts of things occur in any society is determined, in part, by the size of the group involved (often called the "at-risk" group). For example, when there are many children, a society will typically have large school enrollments. When there are many elderly, we can expect the society to have a high rate of heart disease. By the same token, the larger the relative number of unmarried women of childbearing ages, the greater the potential for nonmarital births. The ratio of unmarried to married women hinges, in turn, upon the typical ages of women when they marry. In most societies, at most times, the vast preponderance of people marry. What varies the most is how old they are when they first marry. The older the average age, the larger the at-risk group of unmarried women will likely be at any given time. And finally, the relative proportion of unmarried women in a society depends upon whether women usually remarry quickly after they divorce or become widowed.

Over the past fifty years or so, there have been steady increases in the proportion of women of childbearing ages who are not married. Each of the variables noted has contributed to the increase, and we will discuss each in the following pages. However, showing how the population at risk has increased does not offer a *complete* explanation for why or how the rate increased. Still missing is an account of how people's subjective experiences and relationships with others shaped the individual decisions and actions that, in the aggregate, became the societal rate.

In other words, we regard demographic distributions as reflecting how many at-risk people there are, but not how these people will behave with respect to marriage, childbearing, and the like.[1] If we ignore the technology of modern fertility clinics, it is obvious that for unmarried women to bear children, they must engage in sexual relations without utilizing contraceptives. Either a high level of (imprudent) sexual intimacy when the cohort of unmarried women is small or a low level of intimacy when the cohort is large is sufficient to produce a substantial number of out-of-wedlock conceptions. If the cohort is large and sexual relations (without precautions) are commonplace, then the potential is in place for an exceptionally large number of nonmarital pregnancies. Whether many out-of-wedlock births will actually occur in the society, however, then depends upon how frequently women neither seek an abortion nor quickly marry the father of the child they are carrying.

In sum, if we want to understand the out-of-wedlock birthrate in the contemporary United States (or any society), we have to know the relative size of the unmarried cohort of women who are of childbearing ages. That will be our first topic in this chapter. Then we want to examine the decisions these women make concerning: sexual intimacy, the use of contraceptives, abortion, and pregnancy-driven (i.e., "shotgun") marriages. We must bear in mind that it is only when women make a particular sequence of choices on these matters that nonmarital births result.

THE INCREASE IN UNMARRIED WOMEN

To examine nonmarital births from a demographic perspective, we begin by asking about the relative number of women aged 15 to 44. This span encompasses women's childbearing ages, and the larger the relative size of this group, the higher the fertility rate of any society will be—including both marital and nonmarital births.[2] Given our topic, we focus particularly upon unmarried women between the ages of 15 and 44 years. They are the at-risk cohort, and our first task here is to examine how the relative size of this cohort increased between 1960 and 1995 as a result of older ages at first marriage, higher divorce rates, and delayed remarriages. We will discuss each of these components and then note that the increased size of the unmarried cohort and its greater fertility were one side of an equation that led to a higher *proportion* of out-of-wedlock births. Simultaneously, the other side of the equation was a decline in marital birthrates.

Age at First Marriage

In most societies, at most times, the vast preponderance of people marry. Over the past fity years, between 90 percent and 95 percent of all adults in America got married at some time in their lives. In fact, the percentage of the population who ever marry has, of late, been modestly increasing. The change with the most implications for us is how old people were when they first married. The older that average age, the larger the at-risk cohort of unmarried women will be at any given time. After declining throughout the first half of the twentieth century, the average age at first marriage increased rapidly during the last half of the century, as illustrated in figure 3.1.

There are, no doubt, a large number of variables that have contributed to people marrying later. Increased levels of education have kept everyone in school longer, and as women's occupational and educational aspirations approximated men's, so too did their typical age at marriage. How old people were when they first married also became more a matter of individual choice. Especially for young women, the norms that prescribed early marriage became weaker and more flexible.[3]

Figure 3.1
Median Age at First Marriage

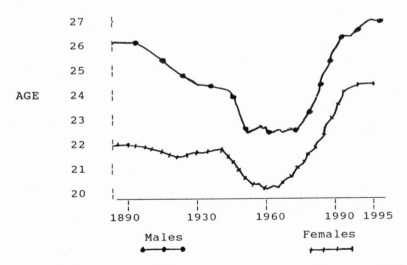

Source: Adapted from Arlene F. Saluter, *Marital Status and Living Arrangements: March 1994*, U.S. Bureau of the Census, Current Population Reports, Population Characteristics P20–484 (Washington, DC: GPO, 1996), table B.

There was also a demystification of marriage, as young people looked around and saw older people who were unhappy, getting divorced. To illustrate, one woman who was born in the 1950s initially had a traditional and romantic view of married life. Her own parents, she later recalled, "were so Ozzie and Harriet. . . . Mother was always preparing breakfast and . . . at the window when we came home." But her older brother married when she was eight years old, and she proceeded to observe him and his wife fighting and screaming at each other. She remembers deciding she would wait and not rush into marriage once she came to realize that married life was not just "calico curtains and picking out silver patterns."[4]

As we noted in the preceding chapter, many marital and childbearing patterns markedly vary among persons from different racial and ethnic groups. This is also true of the distribution of never-married women. The figures, by race and age, for women between the ages of 20 and 44 years are presented in table 3.1.

From looking down each column of numbers in table 3.1, it is clear that, as we would expect, the older a woman is, the more likely it is that she married at some time. Statistics for men, not shown in this table, display the same trend. Looking across the rows in the table, we also see that from decade to decade women in the same age group became more likely never to have married. Among Hispanic women between 20 and 24 years, for example, only one-third had never married in 1970. In contrast, by 1994 well over one-half of the Hispanic women in the 20–24 age group had never married.

While marriage rates declined among women of all races, the racial-ethnic differences were also very pronounced. Specifically, black women of childbearing ages become increasingly more likely never to have married than either white or Hispanic women. By 1994, one-half of all black women did not marry until they were in their early thirties. While black women were markedly different from white and Hispanic women in terms of age at first marriage, differences between the latter were small. More Hispanic than white women married at relatively young ages, but white women soon matched their cumulative rates.

Other data, not summarized in table 3.1, indicate that the decline in marriage may have occurred despite increases in the overall availability of potential marriage partners. While the largest increase in the proportion who never married occurred among the youngest women, there was simultaneously an increase in the relative number of males in the age and educational categories that would have made them eligible mar-

Table 3.1
Percentage of Women Never Married

Ethnicity/Race age	1970	1980	1994
Black			
20 - 24 yrs.	44	69	81
25 - 29 yrs.	19	37	61
30 - 34 yrs.	11	19	43
35 - 39 yrs.	12	12	31
40 - 44 yrs.	7	9	22
Hispanic			
20 - 24 yrs.	33	43	57
25 - 29 yrs.	14	23	32
30 - 34 yrs.	8	11	21
35 - 39 yrs.	7	7	13
40 - 44 yrs.	6	8	10
White			
20 - 24 yrs.	35	47	63
25 - 29 yrs.	9	18	31
30 - 34 yrs.	6	8	16
35 - 39 yrs.	5	5	10
40 - 44 yrs.	5	4	7

Source: Adapted from Arlene F. Saluter, *Marital Status and Living Arrangements: March 1994.* U.S. Bureau of the Census, Current Population Reports, Population Characteristics P20-484 (Washington, DC: GPO, 1996), table C.

riage partners for these young women.[5] There are some differences within the various racial-ethnic groups, and the attractiveness of the available males as marriage partners is a separate issue. Nevertheless, the overall increase in the proportion of never-married women does not appear to be a function of a simple reduction in the number of age-appropriate males.

Divorce and Remarriage

The relative proportion of unmarried women in the United States also depends upon how frequently marriages are terminated by divorce and how quickly women remarry after they divorce or become widowed. Among women under age 30, the rate of divorce following first marriages changed little between the 1970s, and 1990s. To be more specific, there was a large increase in younger women's divorce rates during the 1970s, and it was followed by a small decrease in the 1980s, so the overall change for women under age 30 was small. However, among women over age 30, after 1970 there was an unbroken increase in the percent who divorced after a first marriage, and the largest increase occurred in the 1970s. During this peak, interviewers in a midwestern city documented how much housewives' attitudes toward marriage and divorce had changed since their mothers' days. The women of the 1970s regarded easier divorces as part of the new women's rights, and stressed that there were new-found limits to what they would pay just to be able to have a husband. As one respondent explained the change, "Women don't have to put up with their [husbands'] crap—they can support themselves."[6]

Two other related post-1970 trends are highly pertinent to our current discussion: (1) the percentage of women who remarried after obtaining a divorce consistently declined, and (2) the percentage of women who redivorced after remarrying consistently increased. During this period divorce and remarriage among men followed essentially the same trends.[7] After obtaining a divorce, many people claimed that they felt much more autonomous and that they enjoyed the feeling, especially after suffering a loss of freedom in their marriages. Why then rush into another marriage? As one woman, a 33-year-old schoolteacher, explained it, "After my divorce . . . I liked not being responsible to anyone, just being in charge of myself. I realized the limits that a marriage places on that."[8]

In sum, at any given time, the proportion of American women aged 15 to 44 who are in marital relationships—that is, whose current marital status is married—has more or less continuously declined during the past twenty-five years. The main contributor to the decline has been the growing percentage of (mostly younger) women who have never been married, but higher rates of divorce, lower rates of remarriage, and higher rates of redivorce also play a part. The net effect has been that a growing segment of the female population of childbearing ages became at risk with respect to out-of-wedlock births, and the largest segment among them was comprised of relatively young, never-married women.

We should also note that during the 1970s, as the age at first marriage was increasing and divorce was becoming more commonplace, marital fertility rates plummeted. To be more specific, between 1970 and 1976, birthrates among married women ages 15 to 44 declined by about 25

percent. Their rates then fluctuated up and down over a very small range over the next fifteen years or so. During the first half of the 1990s, births to married women consistently declined, by small amounts, from year to year.[9] Thus over this twenty-five-year period, marital fertility rates came down, while nonmarital fertility rates went up.

Choosing Cohabitation (Over Marriage)

The Bureau of the Census defines cohabiting unions as those in which an unmarried man and woman are living together. In many respects they are marriagelike relationships, though there appear to be some consistent differences. For example, a number of studies indicate that cohabiting couples are less likely to follow traditional gender roles than married couples. Thus the contributions of men and women to housework are more equal among cohabitants. In addition, opportunities for separate and independent lives tend to be valued more by cohabitant than by married couples. Thus they tend to disapprove less strongly of infidelity.[10]

Over the last twenty-five years or so, cohabiting households have been increasing by more than 100,000 per year. More meaningful, perhaps, is the fact that the proportion of households that consist of an unmarried (i.e., cohabiting) couple has been increasing in frequency relative to married-couple households. To be specific, in 1970 there was only 1 unmarried couple for every 100 who were married; there were 3 per 100 in 1980, 5 per 100 in 1990, and by 1993 there were 6 per 100.[11]

The percentage of cohabiting households that contained children under age 15 declined between 1970 and 1980, corresponding with a rapid increase in the proportion of young and childless couples who formed nonmarital households. From 1980 to the mid-1990s, however, the percentage of cohabiting households with children under 15 years steadily increased. This was a result of two distinct processes: first, some of the cohabiting couples became parents but did not marry; second, some adults with children from prior relationships formed new nonmarital households and brought their children with them.

About 25 percent of all stepfamilies contain an (unmarried) cohabiting couple and a child (or children). In fact, about 35 percent of these households formed following a nonmarital birth. And of all stepfamilies in which the parents are married, one-half began as cohabiting unions. What makes these figures especially important is the fact that many of the people in these cohabiting stepfamilies probably act exactly like people in marital families, which makes them sociologically different from many single-parent families. However, many official statistics cannot differentiate between a household comprised of an unmarried mother and her children and a cohabiting stepfamily. Larry Bumpass and R. Kelly Raley estimate that the increase in the number of mother-only households that is tabulated in census and other reports is exaggerated by about 20 percent because of the inability of the statistics to separate out the cohabiting two-partner households.[12]

Who will choose to cohabit and who will choose to marry raises an interesting question. William Axinn and Arland Thornton propose that marriage and cohabitation be viewed as competing ways in which people leave single life behind, and they analyzed the variables that predisposed people to select one versus the other. Their data came from interviewing seven waves of respondents who were representative of the Detroit area between 1961 and 1985. The analysis showed that mothers' background and attitudes exerted important influences upon their offsprings' decisions to cohabit or marry, and upon the decisions of their daughters, in particular. Thus, young women were more likely to cohabit and less likely to marry when their mothers believed that cohabitation was all right. Because they had data on the same people over time, Axinn and Thornton were able to show that a mother's attitudes preceded her daughter's actions, and hence were one of the important variables pushing her daughter down one path or the other.[13]

Interestingly, the investigators also showed that when daughters did cohabit, their mothers' general attitudes toward cohabitation subsequently became more favorable and permissive, regardless of their former view. I think this change occurs because of the importance many mothers attach to maintaining a close relationship with their grown daughters. When a daughter's cohabitation plan runs counter to her mother's value system and the mother cannot dissuade the daughter from pursuing a nonmarital relationship, the mother strives to accommodate to the situation by modifying her own values. In so doing, the mother eliminates a potential obstacle to continuing a close relationship with her daughter. Independent of and in addition to mothers' attitudes, the research also showed that children's cohabitation, rather than marriage, was encouraged by the mothers' own (prior) familial experiences. Thus, mothers who were divorced or widowed or who had a premarital pregnancy raised children, and daughters especially, who had higher rates of nonmarital cohabitation.[14]

CHOICES

We turn now to an examination of how decisions made by women in the expanded cohort of unmarried women translate into nonmarital births. Figure 3.2 shows a series of choice points—connected by a line—that can lead to an out-of-wedlock birth. *Any* deviation from the one combination of choices connected by the line is sufficient to prevent a nonmarital birth from occurring.

When the line continues between choice events, as displayed in figure 3.2, it indicates that a woman remains "on track" for a nonmarital birth.[15] At any point prior to delivery, the woman can terminate the process; for example, if upon learning that she is pregnant the woman chooses to have an abortion, then the line ends there. If a woman abstains from sexual relations, then of course the process never begins.

Intercourse without Marriage

In the preceding pages we reviewed how the number of unmarried women (and men) in the society at any given time increased. Involvement in sexual activities—the first variable in figure 3.2—has not been similarly delayed or postponed, though. To the contrary, in fact, it has increased, especially among young, never-married females.

Premarital Relations

Among adolescents younger than age 15, there have been only small across-time differences in the percentage who are sexually active, be-

Figure 3.2
Choices Preceding Out-of-Wedlock Births

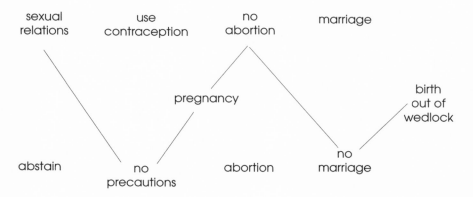

cause rates of involvement are very low in every time cohort. Fewer than 20 percent of 15-year-olds in any cohort have been sexually active. Among 16-year-olds, a trend toward increased sexual intercourse begins to become visible, and among 18- and 19-year-olds, the trend is very clear. Table 3.2 presents data for three cohorts of teenagers who reached age 18 in different decades.

Two trends stand out in table 3.2. Note first that sexual activity among both males and females increased between time periods. In other words, by age 18 teenagers became increasingly likely to have engaged in sexual intercourse. Second, note that the proportional increase was much greater among females, and that in the cohort that most recently turned 18 years old, gender differences were almost nonexistent.

Not shown in table 3.2 are the marked racial and educational differences that have been reported among adolescents. In chapter 2 we described the large differences in rates of out-of-wedlock births between blacks and whites and among women with varying levels of education. Part of those differences is due to the greater sexual precociousness of black females. Studies report black females' first intercourse, on average, occurs nearly one year earlier than white females' first intercourse. Why this difference occurs, however, has been explained in very different ways. Some studies have stressed the importance of physiological differences, such as black females' earlier maturation. A large number of studies have reported a later average onset of sexual activity among both black and white youngsters from higher socioeconomic families. Earlier sexual experiences among blacks than whites are then perhaps explained by the lower average educational and occupational attainments of blacks. In addition, even after many background characteristics are held

Table 3.2
Percentage Experiencing Intercourse by Age 18

Cohort Turned Age 18 Between	Male	Female
1981 and 1992	61%	58%
1971 and 1980	57%	48%
1961 and 1970	48%	30%

Source: From Edward O. Laumann, John Gagnon, Robert T. Michael, and Stuart Michaels, *The Social Organization of Sexuality* (Chicago: University of Chicago Press, 1994), appendix table IV–1.

constant in analyses, blacks are still found to have a greater tendency than whites to enter cohabiting unions rather than marry.[16] Their higher out-of-wedlock rates are, therefore, partially due to higher rates of informal cohabitation rather than formal marriage.

Finally, the isolated inner-city neighborhoods in which many blacks live may afford youngsters limited opportunities to directly observe stable married couples raising families. The adolescents' expectations for their own futures may be shaped by these observations, resulting in little constraint against rushing into adult sexual behaviors. Why not? What, they may ask, do they have to lose?[17]

Extramarital and Nonmarital Relations

A number of surveys have asked married or previously married persons to disclose their extramarital or nonmarital sexual activities. What these studies report varies greatly, depending upon how the research is conducted. Some studies have claimed extensive increases in people's rates of involvement in sexual affairs outside of marriage by comparing the self-reports of older and younger respondents. Not only is it questionable whether people remember equally well, but many of these surveys have been very poorly done methodologically. First, they have asked people to respond to ambiguous questions about their sexual experiences, so it is difficult to interpret what the responses mean. Second, the samples have been selected in dubious ways. For example, the readers of a particular magazine have been asked to tear out a questionnaire, fill it out, and mail it in, or the members of certain types of organizations have been asked to volunteer to be interviewed. Because samples of this type are not representative of any meaningful population, their results are difficult to interpret and impossible to compare to other samples.[18]

The more reliable studies suggest that there has been an increase in extramarital sexual contact over the last half of the twentieth century, though not to the degree implied by many of the studies that relied upon dubious samples.[19] Furthermore, in surveys with representative samples, almost all respondents continue to condemn marital unfaithfulness. For example, in 1994, 89 percent of the population still thought it was always or almost always wrong for a married person to have sexual relations with someone other than the marriage partner.[20]

An interesting anomaly remains with respect to laws governing adultery, however. In about one-half of the states, a married person is still guilty of adultery if he or she has an extramarital affair. In some states (e.g., Arizona and Maryland), it is a misdemeanor, but in others (e.g.,

Massachusetts and Wisconsin), it can be a felony. However, adultery is almost never prosecuted, and even if an enraged spouse swears out a complaint, formal charges are usually dismissed.[21] Therefore, while most people express disapproval of unfaithfulness, at least in the abstract, that disapproval is not effectively backed up by a readiness to punish people who deviate from the ideal.

Contraceptive Use

Let us begin by stating the obvious: unless people take precautions, sexual intercourse will often lead to pregnancy. If not terminated, pregnancy will usually lead to childbirth, and if the woman is not married, then the birth will be out of wedlock. We have already discussed the increase in the proportion of unmarried (at-risk) women and seen that sexual activity outside of marriage has begun earlier and become more widespread. Despite these trends, an increase in out-of-wedlock births could still be prevented without shotgun marriages by widespread utilization of contraceptive techniques (or by abortion).

It is not easy to calculate the rate of unplanned or unwanted pregnancies. It would be best to question women as soon as they became pregnant, but obtaining a representative sample of such women would present a formidable task. As a concession to practical impediments, researchers usually ask the question about planning retroactively to women after the birth of a child. Two forces then conspire to lead women to deny that any child was unplanned. First, a woman may be embarrassed to admit that she did not rationally plan her family. Second, given the presence of an actual child that she loves, the mother may find it very difficult to confess, even to herself, that at one time she did not want this child. We can reasonably assume, therefore, that statistics on unplanned pregnancies understate their actual prevalence.

Despite pressures to underestimate, surveys still typically report that 70–80 percent of all pregnancies of unmarried women are unplanned, compared to less than half of the pregnancies of married women. For example, data from one survey, conducted in 1988, reported that nearly 90 percent of the pregnancies to never-married women were unintended, compared to about 70 percent of the pregnancies to previously (but not now) married women. Among women who were married at the time of the survey, the reported rate of unintended pregnancies was 40 percent.[22]

This high rate of unintended pregnancies has multiple causes. Many women, for starters, possess faulty information about fertility. For example, sexually active adolescent females frequently report that they rely upon "time of the month" to prevent pregnancies. When questioned, however, many cannot accurately identify the time when sexual intercourse would be the safest. Another reason for low contraceptive utilization is misinformation about the risks of various methods. Telephone polls and surveys at clinics involving economically and racially diverse samples of women show widespread (and erroneous) beliefs that birth-control pills and IUDs carry serious health risks, such as cancer. And finally, many women dramatically underestimate the efficacy of various contraceptive methods.[23]

Sex-education classes in schools have, over the past decades, been offered more widely and to younger students. They may accomplish some meaningful objectives, but they have apparently been of limited value in preventing teen pregnancies. One young woman who took sex education in school—but nevertheless became pregnant at age 14 with a child she did not want—offered the following view of her former sex-education classes: "They tell you how *to* get pregnant but they don't tell how *not* to get pregnant." [24]

There are also a number of adolescent girls who systematically seem to deny reality and passively view sexual intercourse without contraceptive use as one of the many unplanned aspects of their lives that they must accept. A 17-year-old named Tracy, who lived in a crowded trailer with her baby, parents, and younger brother, is illustrative. While in high school, when Tracy was about to become intimate with her boyfriend, Earl, she asked him to use a condom. He refused, but she still engaged in intercourse with him for a period of months. She sometimes worried about becoming pregnant, but nevertheless continued to be intimate. When at age 16 she did become pregnant, Earl dumped her, and she refused to consider either abortion or adoption as alternatives. She chose to let fate have its way with her, and after her son was born, she and the baby moved into her parents' trailer.

Tracy's aspirations for a better life in the future continue to exhibit the same lack of realistic strategies that characterized her hopes in the past. Her specific dreams have changed because of her obligations to her son, she says, but dreaming continues to dominate over rational planning. Now her main goal is to win the state lottery. Failing that, despite her limited education, poor cognitive skills, and dislike of school, she nevertheless aspires to become a child psychologist.[25]

Abortion

About one-half of all unintended pregnancies, it is estimated, are terminated by abortion. Many women are delighted to discover they are pregnant, even if it was unintended, and there would be no reason for them to consider an abortion. Not all of the women who are displeased seek abortions, for a lot of reasons. Some women refuse to recognize the initial signs that they are pregnant. Tracy, introduced above, suspected that she was pregnant right away. But Earl kept saying, "No you're not, don't worry about it," so, she recalls, "I just kept putting it out of my head." [26] If women do not realize they are pregnant until after the first trimester, when abortions are no longer legal, many then fear the legal and/or medical complications that might arise. Limited access to an abortion clinic—for example, because one does not live in a metropolitan area—can also be discouraging. Still other people (especially born-again Protestants) reject abortions on religious or moral grounds.

There have been two large-scale examinations of abortion patients, both under the auspices of the Guttmacher Institute in Washington, D.C. The surveys, conducted in 1987 and in 1995, entailed analyses of questionnaires given to thousands of women who (at each time period) had abortions in hospitals, clinics, and doctors' offices.[27] Both surveys found that unmarried women were the patients in a much larger percentage of cases than their absolute size would predict. Thus, the use of abortions by unmarried women has kept nonmarital birthrates from growing even larger. Further, it was those groups of unmarried women who had the highest out-of-wedlock rates that were most inclined to seek abortions, namely, blacks and women in the lowest income groups. Thus, if not for this selectivity in abortion utilization, differences in rates of out-of-wedlock births among various segments of the population would apparently be even more pronounced.

Beginning in the early 1970s, when abortion was legalized, induced abortions became increasingly common, and at their peak, in 1983, terminated over 40 percent of all pregnancies. Then, through most of the remainder of the 1980s, there were declines in both the percentage of pregnant women who had abortions (the rate) and the ratio of pregnancies terminated by abortion to live births. From the late 1980s through the mid-1990s, rates and ratios have been largely stable. However, among teenagers, abortion utilization has continued to decline, or the percentage of nonmarital births to teenagers would have fallen even more.[28]

The decline in teenage abortion utilization suggests that progressively fewer unmarried 15 to 19 year olds are regarding abortion as the solution to a pregnancy. In part this may be due to the efforts of fundamentalists and religious conservatives to convince young people that abortion is morally wrong regardless of their circumstances. That belief would of course lead more women to carry fetuses conceived out of wedlock to term. Another part of the decreased use of abortion to terminate teenage pregnancies is probably due to what Bumpass has termed "the declining significance of marriage."[29] Neither parenting nor sex, he argues, now requires the legitimation of marriage: few people object to sexual intimacy among unmarried persons (as long as it is not just a casual relationship), and a majority of the adult population no longer believes that it is necessarily wrong for an unmarried woman to have a child. The impetus to seek abortions, therefore, is weakened.

A few communities have tried to chastise pregnant teenagers, and while the jury is still out on these efforts, they do not seem likely to spread or have much effect. For example, in Gem County (outside Emmett), Idaho, teachers, family members, and social workers have been encouraged to report pregnancies among unmarried teenagers to the office of the county's prosecuting attorney. The girl, or the couple if the father is also known, is charged with fornication under an Idaho law that dates to 1921 and forbids sex between any unmarried persons. Most of the young people in Gem County clearly never heard about this crime, though. A reporter for the *New York Times* asked a group of cheerleaders from the local high school about this law as they were waiting to board a school bus. "Forn-if-cation?" one 17-year-old girl repeated. "What's that?"[30]

The Civil Liberties Union of Idaho has opposed these prosecutions, contending that they are too selective because only teenagers are being charged. (Possible adult violations are ignored.) Other community groups think the lost sense of shame ought to stay lost. "She's pregnant; why make her criminal?" they ask. Given the diverse opposition to the prosecutions, their future in Gem County is very uncertain, and no neighboring Idaho communities are poised to follow this county's lead.

SEPARATING PREGNANCY AND MARRIAGE

From the preceding discussion of the declining significance of marriage, we should not be surprised to find that nonmarital pregnancies have become less likely to act as a signal to people to marry, and in chapter 2 we noted that first births before first marriages became increasingly common in every racial-ethnic group. Shotgun marriages have declined, but they are not entirely a phenomenon of the past. In this section we will review the trends and the results of studies showing which characteristics of unmarried women make them more or less likely to marry when they become pregnant.

There is, of course, no foolproof way to know how many couples may have married to prevent a nonmarital birth. The most widely used approach entails counting the months between birth and marriage. (In most instances the focus is upon first births and first marriages.) If marriage and birth records indicate a birth occured within seven months of a marriage, the marriage is conventionally regarded by researchers as "legitimating" the child.[31] While this seems to be the best measure, errors do creep in from both sides. On the one hand, premature births inflate the figure. On the other hand, shotgun marriages are underestimated when pregnancies led to marriages but not births because of miscarriages, which terminate nearly 10 percent of all pregnancies. There is also the special case of people who marry because they believe that the woman is pregnant, but they are incorrect and no birth results. Despite the shortcomings, counting the months between marriage and birth is still the best way to estimate pregnancy-driven marriages within the society.

Allan Parnell and associates examined several waves of respondents from a number of longitudinal surveys. By combining the various survey samples, the investigators were able to do a thorough analysis of respondents' life experiences between the middle 1950s and the middle 1980s. They found five variables to be the most significant, among both blacks and whites, in disposing pregnant but unmarried females to marry *before* they gave birth. (That is, their children were born within seven months of their marriages.)[32] The five variables are:

1. Education. Failure to complete high school was associated with much lower likelihoods of marrying. This is the culmination of a series of ways in which low educational attainments lead to high out-of-wedlock birthrates. As we have noted, the process begins when females with less education engage in sexual intercourse at an earlier age.

2. Age. Girls who were 15 or younger when they became pregnant were especially unlikely to marry before their child was born.

3. Family background. Girls who were brought up by both parents (i.e., had two parents in their household when they were age 14) were much more likely to marry if they conceived prior to marriage.

4. Marital expectations. Those females who said they expected, prior to the time of their conception, that they would marry while they were still young were found to be more likely to marry after becoming pregnant. (Perhaps they thought marriage was likely because they were already in a meaningful relationship when asked about their plans?)

5. Southern background or residence. Especially among white women, those who were living in or were brought up in a southern state were more likely to marry if they became pregnant. This may be a reflection of generally more traditional southern values, or maybe southerners simply have less access to abortion clinics.

These variables, as we have noted, operate to influence marital probabilities among never-married black and white women who become pregnant. However, for nonwhite females, the probabilities of marriage—regardless of education, family background, or the like—are almost always substantially lower than for white females. And *everyone's* probability of marriage following an out-of-wedlock conception has declined since the 1960s.

The racial differences, the historical trend, and the impact of other major variables are all illustrated in table 3.3. This table intentionally includes only the females who are the "worst" marriage candidates. None of them lived with both parents at age 14, all of them had a first birth at age 16 or 17, and none of them completed high school.[33]

As table 3.3 makes clear, the pregnant young black women who had the odds of pregnancy leading to marriage before birth stacked against them throughout the entire period had virtually no chance of marrying by the 1980s. The once coercive power of pregnancy as a signal to marriage is illustrated by the fact that in the 1960s even among young white women whose pregnancy was least likely to lead to marriage before they gave birth, two-thirds still married before they became mothers. The

Table 3.3
Worst Candidates' Probabilities of Marriage before Birth

	White	Black
1960s	68%	26%
1970s	58%	14%
1980s	22%	<1%

Source: Data from Allan M. Parnell, Gray Swicegood, and Gilian Stevens, "Nonmarital Pregnancies and Marriage in the United States," *Social Forces*, 73, Sept. 1994.

steep decline in this figure suggests that among the worst of the white marital candidates, pregnancy will soon exert no impetus to marriage before a child is born. And again we see a situation in which black patterns are replicated among whites later in time.

THE FATHERS

Throughout this chapter we have paid primary attention to describing the women who become unmarried mothers. We know much less about the males who father out-of-wedlock children. Because census and survey operatives encounter many more mothers than fathers when they canvass neighborhoods, it is a great deal easier to obtain information about mothers. Further, if a sampled household contains multiple children fathered by different men, then there is no way to readily describe *a* father's characteristics. There are no firm, reliable data on the proportion of multiple-children households headed by a never-married mother that involve children with different fathers. Estimates from small studies suggest that in about one-half of all such households, the children had two or more different fathers. Focusing upon the men, it also appears that about one-half (or more) of unmarried men who have fathered multiple children may have done so with different mothers.[34] And finally, we should note that descriptions of fathers are often limited to the data that can be obtained from surveys, because in many states it is not legal to include any information about the baby's father on the birth certificate if the parents are not married.

It is, of course, typically the mother and not the father who remains with children when a nonmarried couple split up (or a marriage dissolves). In 1993, approximately 85 percent of all families with children and one never-married parent were headed by a female rather than a male householder. However, as shown in table 3.4, when the never-married householder had two or more children or was under age 20, then the never-married householder was especially likely to be a woman.

Census Bureau projections suggest that the overall proportion of female-headed one-parent families may decline in the next century. The total number of one-parent families and their percentage of all families with children are both expected to increase, but it is the proportion headed by men that seems likely to rise. By the year 2010, the bureau projects that male householders will comprise approximately 25 percent of all one-parent families with children. (This will include men who never married plus men who were separated, divorced, or widowed.)[35]

Table 3.4
Never-Married One-Parent Family Households by Gender of Householder,
1993 (in Thousands)

	With Any Children	One Child Only	Two or More Children	Parent under Age 20
Male Head	412	255	157	9
Female	2,275	1,132	1,142	110

Source: Data from Steve W. Rawlings, *Household and Family Characteristics: March 1993*, U.S. Bureau of the Census, Current Population Reports P20–477 (Washington, DC: GPO, 1993), table 9.

Much of the information we have concerning the fathers of children born out of wedlock is partial and limited. For example, we have information about fathers' ages from one national study of nearly 10,000 women who gave birth in 1988. The findings showed that the younger the age of the mother, the more the father was likely to be substantially older. To be specific, among females aged 15 to 17 who had a child—and mothers at this age were almost never married—about 60 percent of the fathers were more than three years older than the mother; nearly 20 percent were six or more years older. By contrast, among women in their 30s, only about 33 percent of the fathers were three or more years older than the mother.[36]

There are also a number of studies conducted in a single state that have reported very similar patterns with respect to age. For example, a Washington State survey of 12- to 17-year-old mothers reported that the average age of the fathers of their babies was 24 years. A large study in California similarly found that when mothers were in their early teens, fathers were, on average, nearly seven years their senior.[37]

In earlier chapters of this book, we encountered anecdotal evidence of this pattern of difference in parents' ages. In chapter 1 we discussed Ernestine Pallet, at age 16, living with her 22-year-old boyfriend, Eugene, in Paris, in 1878. In chapter 2 we introduced Crystal, who at age 14 was living with Daquan, her 23-year-old boyfriend. When confronted by age differences this large, especially when very young girls are involved, one is certainly tempted to wonder whether there is a coercive quality to these relationships. The mismatch in the ages of the pair may suggest that men in their twenties are pressuring girls in their teens into sexual relations, and perhaps into premature motherhood as well. The previously discussed studies on the West Coast as well as another study in Chicago all reported that over 60 percent of the youngest mothers suffered physical and sexual abuse at the hands of older males. In many instances the young girl's pregnancy was due to such an assault.[38]

In a number of other small surveys, investigators have tried to isolate the distinguishing characteristics of unwed fathers. This population is very difficult to identify, though, and the samples selected by researchers have been flawed, limiting the generalizability of these studies. Some have intentionally included only young fathers, for example, while other studies tried to select more diverse sets of respondents, but in ways that could have introduced bias.

We cannot do better now than to offer some highly tentative conclusions from the results of several limited studies. Specifically, it appears that the never-married fathers tend, like the never-married mothers, to have completed only high school educations or less, and they tend disproportionately to be black rather than white.[39] We will return to a more detailed examination of these fathers in chapter 7 when we consider the effects of male joblessness on marriage rates in inner cities.

NOTES

1. For further discussion, see Susan A. McDaniel, "Toward a Synthesis of Feminist and Demographic Perspectives on Fertility," *The Sociological Quarterly*, 37, Winter 1996.

2. Fluctuations in rates that are due to changes in the relative size of particular cohorts are termed "compositional." It is important to identify compositional effects because they tend to be ephemeral, enduring only until offsetting distributional changes occur in the future. Rate changes that are not due to compositional effects, by contrast, have a greater likelihood of enduring. So, it is impossible to fully analyze a trend unless one knows how much of an observed change is "merely" a compositional effect. In addition, one cannot meaningfully compare rates in different societies or across time unless distributional differences are also taken into account. Thus, for figures to be most meaningful, they must either be limited to the at-risk segment of a society or be adjusted for its relative size. This adjustment process is known as "standardization." For further discussion, see Prithwis Das Gupta, *Standardization and Decomposition of Rates*, Bureau of the Census, Current Population Reports, P23-186, Washington, DC: GPO, 1993.

3. See the discussion of these changes in Andrew Cherlin, *Marriage, Divorce, and Remarriage* (Cambridge, MA: Harvard University Press, 1992).

4. Quoted in Kathleen Gerson, *Hard Choices* (Berkeley: University of California Press, 1985), pp. 62–63.

5. Qian Zhenchao and Samuel Preston, "Changes in American Marriage, 1972 to 1987," *American Sociological Review*, 58, June 1993.

6. Theodore Caplow, et al., *Middletown Families* (Minneapolis: University of Minnesota Press, 1982), p. 131.

7. Arthur J. Norton and Louisa F. Miller, *Marriage, Divorce, and Remarriage in the 1990s*, Current Population Reports, P23-180, Bureau of the Census, (Washington, DC: GPO, October 1992).

8. Quoted in Gerson, p. 101.

9. For further description of fertility patterns, see Amara Bachu, *Fertility of American Women: June 1994*, Current Population Reports, Series P20-482, (Washington, DC: GPO, 1995), and H. M. Rosenberg, "Births and Deaths: United States, 1995," *Monthly Vital Statistics Report*, Vol. 45, Supp. 2, 1996.

10. See the review of research and the data presented in Marin Clarkberg, Ross M. Stolzenberg, and Linda J. Waite, "Attitudes, Values, and Entrance into Cohabitational versus Marital Unions," *Social Forces*, 74, Dec. 1995.

11. Arlene F. Saluter, *Marital Status and Living Arrangements: March 1994*, U.S. Bureau of the Census, Current Populations Reports, Population Characteristics P20–484 (Washington, DC: GPO, 1996).

12. Larry L. Bumpass and R. Kelly Raley, "Redefining Single-Parent Families," *Demography*, 32, Feb. 1995.

13. William G. Axinn and Arland Thornton, "Mothers, Children and Cohabitation," *American Sociological Review*, 58, April 1993.

14. Ibid.

15. The sequence arbitrarily places the abortion choice before the marriage choice. In fact, however, marriage could occur at any point along this sequence of events.

16. R. Kelly Raley, "A Shortage of Marriageable Men?" *American Sociological Review*, 61, Dec. 1996.

17. See the discussion of such neighborhood effects in Karin L. Brewster, "Race Differences in Sexual Activity among Adolescent Women," *American Sociological Review*, 59, June 1994. See also William J. Wilson, *The Truly Disadvantaged* (Chicago: University of Chicago Press, 1987).

18. See, for example, the critique of the methodology of the Hite Report in "The Depths of Hite," *National Review*, 40, Jan. 1988.

19. See, for example, Laumann, et al., and Robert T. Michael, John H. Gagnon, and Edward O. Laumann, *Sex in America* (Boston: Little, Brown, 1994).

20. Figures from National Opinion Research Center survey, reported by Karlyn Bowman and Everett C. Ladd, "Opinion Pulse," in *The American Enterprise*, 6, July/Aug. 1995, p. 102.

21. For a review of adultery laws, see Richard A. Posner and Katharine B. Silbaugh, *A Guide to America's Sex Laws* (Chicago: University of Chicago Press, 1996).

22. Jacqueline D. Forrest, "Epidemiology of Unintended Pregnancy and Contraceptive Use," *American Journal of Obstetric Gynecology*, 170, Feb. 1994.

23. For a summary of relevant research, see Sarah S. Brown and Leon Eisenberg (Eds.), *The Best Intentions* (Washington, DC: National Academy Press, 1995).

24. Patricia Lunneborg, *Abortion* (Westport, CT: Bergin & Garvey, 1992), p. 7.

25. Kate Maloy and Maggie J. Patterson, *Birth or Abortion* (New York: Plenum Press, 1992).

26. Ibid., p. 200.

27. For reports of these studies, see Stanley K. Henshaw and Jane Silverman, "The Characteristics and Prior Contraceptive Use of U.S. Abortion Patients," *Family Planning Perspectives*, 20, July 1988, and Stanley K. Henshaw, "Abortion Patients in 1994–95" *Family Planning Perspectives*, 28, Aug. 1996.

28. Kristin A. Moore, *Adolescent Sex, Contraception and Childbearing* (Washington, DC: Child Trends, 1995). See also Deborah Bosanko, "Abortion's Slow Decline," *American Demographics*, 17, Sept, 1995.

29. Larry L. Bumpass, "The Declining Significance of Marriage," Madison, WI: NSFH Working Paper #66, 1995, p. 3.

30. *New York Times*, October 28, 1996, p. A10.

31. This is the one way in which the term "legitimation" continues regularly to be used in the literature. However, I think it still implies that without marriage it is the child who is not legitimate, and I find this implication distressing. Therefore, even though there is no parsimonious alternative, the term will not be used in this book except in reference to inheritance rights, as previously noted.

32. Allan M. Parnell, Gray Swicegood, and Gilian Stevens, "Nonmarital Pregnancies and Marriage in the United States," *Social Forces*, 73, Sept 1994.

33. For historical trend data, see also Deanna L. Pagnini and Ronald R. Rindfuss, "The Divorce of Marriage and Childbearing," *Population and Development Review*, 19, Feb. 1993.

34. See, for example, Maureen R. Waller, "Claiming Fatherhood" (paper presented at American Sociological Association, Washington, DC, 1995), and Mary Achatz and Crystal A. MacAllum, *Young Unwed Fathers* (Philadelphia: Public/Private Ventures, 1995).

35. Figures from table 5 in Jennifer C. Day, *Projections of the Number of Households and Families in the United States.* (U.S. Bureau of the Census, Current Population Reports, P25-1129, Washington, DC: GPO, 1996).

36. In interpreting these age differences, take into account that males' first intercourse, on average, occurs when they are about one year younger than females, and on average, males are two years older than the females they marry.

David J. Landry and Jacqueline D. Forrest, "How Old Are U.S. Fathers?" *Family Planning Perspectives*, 27, Jan. 1995.

37. These studies are summarized in *New York Times*, Aug. 2, 1995, p. A10.

38. For further discussion, see Kristin A. Moore, "Nonvoluntary Sexual Activity among Adolescents," *Family Planning Perspectives*, 21, Feb 1989, and Mike Males, "Poverty, Rape, and Adult/Teen Sex," *Phi Delta Kappan*, 75, Fall 1994.

39. See Landry and Forrest, and Janet B. Hardy and Anne K. Duggan, "Teenage Fathers and the Fathers of Infants of Urban, Teenage Mothers," *American Journal of Public Health*, 78, Aug. 1988.

PART 2

COMPARATIVE CASE STUDIES

This section provides a detailed examination of several other places that once experienced rapid increases in their out-of-wedlock birthrates. While we are primarily interested in explaining the contemporary United States, that is (paradoxically) very difficult to do without reference to other societies. Specifically, we would like to be able to offer some statements concerning the relative importance of three potential causes of the recent increase in the United States: a decline in traditional family values, welfare programs that enticed young women into unmarried motherhood, and constricting employment opportunities that prevented people from establishing independent households.

However, it is very difficult to infer how much people's values, welfare benefits, or employment opportunities may have contributed to contemporary increases in out-of-wedlock births in the United States, because all three seem to have kicked in more or less simultaneously after about 1960. Whenever several conditions change at about the same time it is very difficult to disentangle their separate effects. It will be helpful, therefore, to examine other societies in which out-of-wedlock birth rates increased and see whether fluctuations in these rates followed any patterns with respect to changes in the societies' values, benefits provided to single mothers, or overall economic conditions.

Perhaps this review will disclose still other conditions that affect the rate of out-of-wedlock births. Our generalizations will be limited by the fact that we will not be able to sample systematically from any universe of societies at different time periods. Given that we wish to examine societies across both space and time, there is no sampling formula we could follow. From the societies we will examine, however, any consistencies we find may be suggestive with respect to understanding what has been happening in recent years in the United States.

Part 2 contains three case studies. Each was selected following several criteria. First, a good deal of apparently reliable historical demographic information was available concerning each one's out-of-wedlock rates or ratios. Substantial materials were also available with which to describe attitudes and patterns of behavior that may have been pertinent to an examination of out-of-wedlock rates. Each of the three cases comes from a different place in the world and a distinct time period. To a large degree, therefore, we are looking at three independent cases. Specifically, chapter 4 examines County of Essex, England, circa 1600; chapter 5 focuses upon Madrid, Spain, circa 1800; and chapter 6 describes Jamaica, West Indies, circa 1960. Immediately prior to the focal time period, there were also marked variations in out-of-wedlock rates in each of the places. Rates in Essex were extremely low; they were moderately low in Madrid; and they were very high in Jamaica. Despite all of the differences described above, the common thread among the three case studies is that each place experienced a sharp increase in nonmarital births during the period in question.

The descriptions of events and changes in each of the case studies are necessarily selective. Too many things simultaneously occur in any place for us to describe everything. I have endeavored to select the descriptions and accounts that seemed most buttressed by primary data analysis and for which there was the most corroboration, regardless of the theoretical perspective the descriptions supported.

4

County of Essex, England, 1590–1625

The county of Essex is about 30 miles to the east and north of London. It is a modern suburb with residential communities and new research-and-development firms, computer manufacturers, and such international corporations as Ford Motor Company and Shell Oil. In 1993, when Costco (a discount chain headquartered in Seattle) opened, the county of Essex also became home to the first warehouse club in Europe.

Moving back forty years before Costco opened, many parts of the county were relatively undeveloped. At the height of the Cold War, in 1953, the British government built a secret underground headquarters beneath some then-open fields of Essex. The complex was designed to house up to six hundred senior government ministers and their staffs in the event Britain experienced a nuclear attack.[1] Moving back four hundred years, in those same Essex fields, farmers grew wheat, barley, carrots, and other crops. By the late sixteenth century, they were feeding residents of the county and transporting tons of surplus crops for sale in London's growing produce markets.

Near the center of the county is Terling. In the sixteenth and seventeenth centuries, it was a relatively prosperous farming community, whose demographic statistics have been extraordinarily well-preserved. Just after the turn of the seventeenth century, historical records indicate that Terling's out-of-wedlock ratio increased almost tenfold, and this chapter will examine how that dramatic increase occurred. Let us begin, however, with an overview of the village and the county.

ESSEX AND TERLING

In the late sixteenth century, the county of Essex contained over 100 agricultural villages, a mix of small and large farms, some market towns, and a few manufacturing centers. Its largest farms employed dozens of live-in servants and apprentices who worked as cooks, bakers, carpenters, and so forth. They typically ranged in age from young adolescents to men and women in their thirties. About six to eight additional laborers were employed by the large farms to work year-around in the fields or with the livestock. Another twenty to twenty-five field hands, along with the wives of the regular laborers, would be added to the work force seasonally for weeding and harvesting. The small farms, by contrast, were worked by individual families who either owned or rented the land.

Although farming predominated in sixteenth-century Essex, the county was not exclusively agricultural. By the middle of the century, its northern portion was becoming simultaneously industrial and agricultural. Especially notable was Colchester, England's oldest town, located in the northeast corner of Essex. After 1563, immigrants from the Netherlands helped to transform Colchester into a textile-manufacturing center producing and exporting woolen and worsted fabrics made from locally grown flax and hemp.[2]

A road, major by the standards of the day, connected Colchester and London. (That road evolved into a modern expressway connecting Colchester and suburban Essex with London.) Figure 4.1 shows the towns and the road as they appeared circa 1600. All the towns except London were (and are) in the county of Essex. Figure 4.1 is not drawn to scale, however. If it were, the distance between Chelmsford (near the southern tip of the county of Essex) and the city of London would be about three times greater.[3]

The highway from Colchester to London ran less than a mile from the center of Terling, the town that is the primary focus of this chapter. While Terling was a distinct place whose villagers held local get-togethers and went to church and alehouses together, its residents also moved a good deal and had a lot of both social and commercial contacts with people in other towns, especially the towns located on this road (including Colchester and London).

To illustrate the kind of geographic mobility that characterized this period, consider the experience of Robert and Mary Johnson. Their backgrounds are described in court records because officials in Terling interrogated them about the validity of their marriage. Once Robert

Figure 4.1
County of Essex and London, Circa 1600

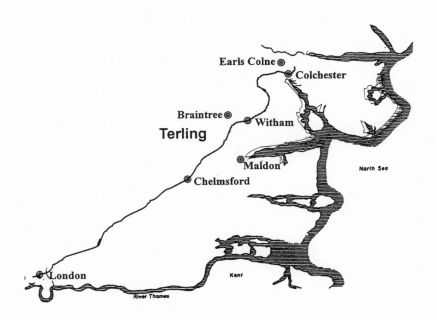

and Mary had been merely nodding acquaintances in a small Essex set-tlement about 20 miles from Terling. Mary and her first husband lived there for more than ten years. Robert lived there for only about one year. During this time he apparently fathered an out-of-wedlock child with an unnamed woman, then he moved alone to London, seeking work as a laborer. There are some gaps in the surviving story, but Mary's first husband apparently died, and a few years later she bumped into Robert at a market. Neither of them was now married. After a brief courtship, she returned with him to London, where they were married. They subsequently moved to Terling for unknown reasons, and in 1603 there is in the town's records a baptism certificate for their daughter, Frances. The Johnsons remained in Terling, where they raised their daughter. In 1625 Frances, now 23 years old, married a Terling laborer, and they eventually had seven children. Three died in infancy, two grew up in Terling and moved elsewhere before they married, and two re-mained to marry in Terling and raise their own families there.[4]

For decades around the turn of the seventeenth century, only about one-third of the couples baptizing a first child in Terling had actually married in the village. Some of the individuals had grown up in Terling, married outside the village in the spouse's town, and then returned to Terling as part of a married couple. However, many married couples simply turn up in the town's records as having been previously married elsewhere, and neither individual appears in earlier registers.

NONMARITAL BIRTHS AROUND 1600

What draws us to Terling and the county of Essex around the turn of the seventeenth century is the dramatic increase that occurred in the proportion of all infants born to women who were not married to the infant's father. Between 1560 and 1590, the total out-of-wedlock ratio in Terling hovered between 1 percent and 2 percent. Parish, church, and court records indicate that beginning just after 1590 the ratio began steadily to increase. It peaked at nearly 10 percent between 1600 and 1610. The proportion of nonmarital births then began steadily to decline. By 1620 it was down to about 6 percent, by 1630 it was about 3 percent, and then it continued to fall more slowly for the rest of the seventeenth century.[5]

Another way to see how dramatic the increase was is to break the 130-year period between 1570 and 1700 into thirteen 10-year intervals. If out-of-wedlock births were evenly distributed across this era, then any 10-year block of time would contain roughly one-thirteenth of the total out-of-wedlock births in Terling. However, about one-third of the entire period's nonmarital births occurred in just one such interval, between 1597 and 1607.[6]

Nonmarital birthrates in Terling (and other Essex towns) are calculated from several sources of data. One consists of parish and church court records, because such births and prenuptial pregnancies were both secular and religious crimes.[7] The distinction was often blurred, but the church courts were primarily concerned with upholding Christian morality, while civic authorities wanted to identify paternity so the community would not bear the expense of providing for a fatherless child. When punishments were meted out by any court, the mother was much more likely than the father to be the target. If the male was prosecuted at all, it was typically to recover some child-support costs. Women, by contrast, faced a hierarchy of court-imposed sanctions: public confession of sins, public whipping (often conducted on market day to ensure a good turnout), confinement to a house of correction, and, in rare instances, hanging.

Almost every infant born in Terling was baptized, regardless of its parents' marital status, and a comparison of baptism certificates with marriage records provides important information with respect to infants' legal status. Specifically, when there is evidence that a marriage occurred but did not precede baptism by eight and a half months or more, the timing permits the inference of a prenuptial pregnancy. Further, when there are records of a baptism but no evidence of a marriage occurring, it probably indicates an out-of-wedlock birth. Finally, by comparing baptism and marriage records to court cases it is also possible to infer the proportion of prenuptial pregnancies and out-of-wedlock births that were prosecuted in either secular or religious courts.

It should be noted, however, that all calculations of out-of-wedlock births in the sixteenth and seventeenth centuries understate the true rate. England's bastardy laws and community opinion gave citizens plenty of incentive to try to hide the existence of such infants. Some desperate women abandoned their newborns behind local churches, at the sides of roads, or at a foundling hospital in London. Other unwed mothers deliberately killed their newborns before they could be baptized and then claimed they had been stillborn. Suspicion that mothers were murdering out-of-wedlock infants grew during the early seventeenth century, and in 1624 England passed a law designed "to prevent the murthering [sic] of bastard children."[8]

From the late 1500s through the middle 1600s, about 80 percent of all recognized out-of-wedlock births appear to have resulted in formal charges being brought, typically against the unwed mother. This high percentage of prosecution implies that throughout the period community leaders had little tolerance of nonmarital childbearing. By contrast, over the last two decades of the sixteenth century and the first decades of the seventeenth, only about 30 percent of nonmarital pregnancies were prosecuted.

It was very common throughout Essex and much of England at this time for a bride to be pregnant on her wedding day. From a comparison of baptismal and marriage records, it appears that between 1550 and 1600 about one in three Terling brides was pregnant. Their condition seems to have been largely tolerated, though—so long as there was a marriage before the child was born. Following the dramatic increase in nonmarital births at the turn of the century, however, Terling's elders became increasingly concerned with prenuptial pregnancy, and about 75 percent of all known cases were brought to the courts after 1620.[9]

On the one hand, the increased prosecution of prenuptial pregnancies reflected the fact that the distinction between nonmarital pregnancy and nonmarital childbearing had diminished in the community. People may have been less inclined to tolerate prenuptial pregnancy for economic reasons. Because they were less certain that the woman would marry before her child was born, they feared she and the child would fall dependent upon the community's charity. On the other hand, the increased prosecution of such pregnancies can also be viewed in moral terms as reflecting a general tightening of social control in Terling. For example, in the late sixteenth and early seventeenth centuries, the alehouses—very popular neighborhood bars that were centers of social life—came under increasingly close scrutiny. There were both new legislation and tighter enforcement of old laws prohibiting drunkenness, brawling, gambling, dancing, and other "immoral activities" within the alehouses.[10]

In order to complete our picture of out-of-wedlock births in Terling, let us examine the characteristics of people who were charged with the offense. While some descriptive information is completely missing, given the centuries that have elapsed, a surprising amount of information is available. To be specific, for the time period 1570 to 1650 in Terling, virtually nothing is known about roughly one-third of the parents of children born out of wedlock. We can make some informed guesses about these people, though. Some of them were surely non-Terling, and possibly non-Essex, residents: pregnant women (with or without male companions) who were passing through town. Perhaps they were searching for work when the woman suddenly delivered. After she gave birth, these unknown people may have quickly moved on and left no traces of themselves other than the birth record. However, some information is missing even when some local women who were unmarried but visibly pregnant were brought to court. They sometimes refused, out of fear or loyalty, to identify the father or explain the circumstances that led to their pregnancy.[11]

Another one-third or so of all out-of-wedlock births during this period can reasonably be described as due to unexpectedly delayed marriages. The parents of the child born out of wedlock considered themselves betrothed, and in many instances they did eventually marry, but unanticipated circumstances forced them to postpone marriage until after the baby's birth. Most commonly this occurred because they lacked the resources with which to establish their own household.

Another sizable number—perhaps one-fifth of all out-of-wedlock births—seem attributable to "coercive liaisons." What we do know for sure is that these were young mothers who had typically never married and were of lower status than the men who impregnated them. The men were older and were frequently married (though obviously not to these young women). Included in this category are the offspring of: masters and their household servants, clerical schoolmasters and their pupils, stepfathers and their wives' daughters, and so forth.[12] The age and status differences between the males and the females imply that the sexual relations resulting in these pregnancies were not purely consensual. In at least some of these cases, there are explicit accounts of rape or blackmail that corroborate the inference of coercion.

Finally, there is a small, but significant, number—perhaps one-seventh of the total nonmarital births—that may be associated with promiscuity or more general deviance. Some of these mothers maintained long-term relationships with their child's (or children's) father, but in defiance of community norms refused to marry. Other mothers in this category were described by neighbors as lazy sluts, or they were known to have worked as prostitutes in disreputable alehouses. Both the mothers and the fathers in this category tended to have frequent brushes with Terling officials for stealing, violating Sabbath ordinances, public drunkenness, and so on.[13] And many of these "deviant" women tended to have multiple out-of-wedlock children, in contrast to women in the delayed marriage or coerced categories, who tended to have only one nonmarital birth.

Between the late sixteenth and the late seventeenth centuries, there were also some marked changes in the characteristics of parents of infants born out of wedlock in Terling. Persons of lower social standing somewhat predominated throughout the period. However, the social positions of unwed parents more closely reflected the status distribution of the entire community through the first decade of the seventeenth century, when the rapid increase in nonmarital births occurred. Rates declined after 1610, and the proportion of such births that involved the poorest of Terling's residents increased. Correspondingly, the proportion of cases involving unambiguous deviance increased, while the relative number of cases that could be considered due to delayed marriages declined.[14] In other words, after 1610 nonmarital births were less often something that happened to all groups in Terling, and more often occurrences that were confined to a deviant, lower-class subgroup.

PLAY, SEX, AND COURTSHIP

In most of England circa 1600, people married late and died young, relatively speaking. As a result, a small percentage of the adult population was married at any given time compared to the percentage that was either single (i.e., never married) or widowed.

Some births were, of course, the result of adulterous liaisons involving married women, but we know little about them because it was usually possible for a married woman to claim that her husband was the father. Many widows were still young enough to conceive, and some did, but their contribution to out-of-wedlock birthrates was very small compared to that of never-married women. Therefore, in this section we will focus upon courtship and premarital sexual activities of younger, never-married women.

Couples were expected to establish their own independent household when they married, and that meant they had to wait until they could afford the basic necessities of married life. Young people from rich families faced no economic obstacles, and a few of the offspring of ordinary people were lucky enough to inherit a small plot of land or receive a dowry while they were still young. However, most young people had to work for years as servants or apprentices before they saved enough to establish their own households. When they finally married, men in England were typically in their mid to late twenties, and women tended to be a couple of years younger.[15] Terling was unexceptional in this regard: At the turn of the seventeenth century, its average age at marriage among men was a little over 25 years, and the average among women was a little under 25 years.

Seeking employment prior to marriage, young people often left the towns in which they were raised, especially if their town offered limited opportunities for work. In Terling, as in many of the more prosperous Essex villages, this produced concentrated numbers of young adults who were under little direct parental control as they went about selecting a mate. And by the time offspring who stayed home acquired the resources with which to marry, many of their parents had already died. Thus, while a parent's authority over a descendant's choice of a spouse was acknowledged in principle, most young people in fact had a good deal of latitude. This freedom was most circumscribed in the wealthiest circles, where concerns with lineage and inheritance led parents to exert more constraints over their offsprings' mate selection.[16]

There were a number of holidays throughout the year which, in almost every English town, were occasions for young people to get together: St. Valentine's Day, May Day and May Eve, Easter Monday and Easter Tuesday, and so forth. These holidays usually included some type of ritual "play" between young men and women. On Easter Monday, for example, men took women's shoes and ransomed them back for kisses. On Easter Tuesday it was the women's turn to be the aggressors. May Eve, like contemporary Halloween, was a time for mischief, but also for young men and women to leave such items as a tree branch or holly as signs of rejection or affection at each other's windows and doors.

Between major holidays, young people came together at local harvest feasts and festivals and informal gatherings. In Terling there were also outdoor dances, weather permitting, in the center of town, and some people regularly assembled in the village's alehouses. The relationships between unmarried adults at holiday gatherings or festivals generally tended to be boisterous and physical: jostling, teasing, and pushing each other. However, the physical contact was not usually construed as sexual, and males and females did not ordinarily pair off at these gatherings.[17] They interacted as members of groups, like a bunch of contemporary young adolescents in a shopping mall on Friday night.

When an unmarried man and woman were attracted to each other, the first step was usually for them to walk and talk together in public, during the day. They had to take great pains to behave in a highly circumspect way, because church and civil laws in England were exceedingly strict on matters of sexual impropriety. The bishops expected even the appearance of immorality to be reported, and accusations were immediately heard in ecclesiastical courts. The burden of proof at these hearings lay with the accused. Suppose, for example, that a neighbor told others he saw an unmarried couple together in a remote area of the village. If rumors grew and people believed the couple had been sexually intimate, church authorities would begin a hearing by demanding that the couple explain the basis of the rumors.[18]

As a relationship became more serious, a couple tended to meet more at night and in private. Most commonly the man went to the woman's room, with the tacit permission of her parents or the master of the house in which she lived and worked. The male suitor usually brought a gift as a token of his affection when he visited. If he were wealthy, it might be a gold piece or a ring; if not, a garter or a corset stay. The man's offering and the woman's acceptance of these gifts were both interpreted as reflecting their serious commitments to each other. In addition, when the giver or recipient of such a gift had strong feelings for the other, the object itself was believed to have special powers in binding each to the other.[19]

Night visits to a woman's room could involve a third party to serve as an intermediary if a relationship needed a little outside help or to provide supportive testimony if the couple was later accused of sexual misconduct. In other instances a friend of either the man or the woman might be hidden in the room, without the knowledge of the other, in order to witness whether the man proposed marriage.

Kissing and fondling were often parts of these night visits, and as relationships progressed, mutual masturbation apparently became common.[20] Sexual intercourse was usually reserved for couples in the most serious relationships, that is, those who were moving close to marriage. However, once a man promised marriage to a woman—and she believed him—they apparently were very likely to begin to engage in intercourse. Given the lack of contraceptive technology at this time, pregnancies often resulted. Sometimes the woman's pregnancy acted like a warning to the man to leave town in a hurry, but more often it prompted the couple to move up their wedding day so that her condition would not be too obvious before they married.

In principle, some people considered abortion a preferable alternative to marriage, but no effective means for inducing abortion were generally available. There were only folk remedies, which some Essex women employed with occasional success. For example, they vigorously exercised while wearing tight girdles or purchased "rough herbs" in London that were known to be powerful laxatives. There are also a few recorded cases in which a man or his friends intentionally roughed up his pregnant girlfriend in hopes that the beating would lead to a miscarriage.[21]

MARRIAGE

For decades before and after the turn of the seventeenth century, marriage for most people had to be understood as an economic partnership as well as a personal and sexual relationship. For the tiny elite class, marriages solidified the power and holdings of family dynasties. For almost everyone else, marriage meant actively working together to feed a family. In rural areas, wives joined husbands in planting crops and preparing harvests for market. In urban areas, wives worked in the shop with their craftsman husbands, did piecework rate for their husbands' employers, or took part-time jobs picking stones, washing clothes, serving beer in an alehouse, and so forth. Because of their joint contributions to subsistence, according to Wrightson, marriages entailed more "companionate" relationships than the official expressions of male authority at the time would have led one to expect.[22]

The importance of the economic division of labor in marriage may have been at least partly responsible for the explicitly economic negotiations that sometimes occurred between the would-be groom and the bride-to-be's parents or guardians. One typical meeting of this type in the early seventeenth century involved a farmer and his daughter, Christian, who were formally visited by her suitor, Walter, and his older sister. The four of them sat around the fire, ate, and drank, and then Walter asked for Christian's hand in marriage. Her father said it was okay with him. Then, believing his future father-in-law to be rich, Walter asked if he would help support the two of them for ten years. Taken aback because he felt that Walter was asking too much, the farmer reminded him that he had children other than Christian to whom he had responsibilities. They finally compromised on two years of support plus 10 pounds, and the farmer's good-faith promise to do more later if his circumstances permitted.[23]

When everyone agreed to a marriage and the terms, there were a number of ways in which a couple might actually marry. Church canons in 1604 required that a couple's intention to marry be announced ("publishing the banns") in their parish church for three successive services. This gave disappointed suitors, deserted spouses, and others an opportunity to object. If the banns passed and it appeared that neither bride nor groom had been previously married or precontracted to marry another and that they were not related by birth, the officiating cleric could then marry them. (If under age 21, parents' consent was also required.) A couple attempting to marry who was thought to have violated any of the above requisites could be charged with adultery, whoredom, or incest and remanded to ecclesiastical courts for punishment. The publication of the banns was also considered an appropriate time for townspeople to tease and taunt the couple. Much of the joking was directed at the future bridegroom, in particular, and was sexual in nature. The public joking and attention had the function, John Gillis claims, of symbolically separating the pair from the rest of the community of unmarried adults. In addition, because church bells were rung with the publication of the banns, it became difficult for people to change their minds after the announcement. To back out then was defined as an offense against the church.[24]

Some of the pomp and ceremony of medieval weddings remained commonplace in English weddings throughout the seventeenth century. The costs of entertaining friends, relatives, and townspeople clearly overwhelmed the budgets of ordinary people, but even poor villagers frequently went into great debt to put on an impressive show. Civic officials condemned the practice as wasteful, and church authorities denounced the paganism. These customs were very slow to die, though. From Essex villages between 1550 and 1650 there were numerous accounts of families of modest means buying their daughters extravagantly expensive gowns and providing guests with favors, such as gloves and ribbons, and abundant quantities of meat, bread, and ale.[25]

Big weddings were not for everyone, of course. People with something to hide or those in a hurry could avoid potential embarrassment or the risk of detention associated with three church announcements if they had a little money. They could purchase a license and marry immediately and surreptitiously in a morning ceremony in their parish. Other couples went to a cleric in a nearby town who, for a small fee, would marry them without asking too many questions. They might remain in this town for a day or forever, and given the large amount of geographical mobility that was occurring at this time, the presence of newcomers in the community was not, in itself, grounds for suspicion.

CALAMITIES STRIKE

To properly understand the peak in out-of-wedlock rates around the turn of the seventeenth century, they must be viewed as a culmination of several long-term trends. To begin, in the sixteenth century, people became better able to control the epidemics that had previously ravaged their societies. As a result, between about 1520 and 1600, there was extremely high population growth in Terling (as in Essex, England, and much of western Europe). The population growth increased the demand for food, but did not lead to a rise in production. The obvious result was a rampant escalation in the cost of food and other items, but unfortunately, most workers' compensation did not simultaneously increase. It is impossible to calculate the precise loss in purchasing power of the bulk of Essex's population, because monetary payments were a small part of the compensation of servants, farm laborers, apprentices, and other workers. The value of their room and board or their share of the crops is difficult to quantify. More precise estimates can be offered for occupational groups that received wages, such as building craftsmen in southern England. Their experiences were probably illustrative of those of many other workers, and their financial records have been well preserved. From an analysis of these documents, it appears that the craftsmen's wages relative to prices declined in almost every decade from 1500 to 1600, and that the overall deterioration in their purchasing power during the century was about 60 percent.[26]

The population increase also placed inflationary pressures on the land as more people competed for parcels to farm. Large landowners in particular prospered, as they subdivided their acres into smaller and smaller plots that they leased at higher and higher rates. The small farmers soon found themselves in untenable positions. The profits they might make from good harvests were wiped out by mounting rents, and when harvests were bad, they had to buy food (at inflated prices) and fell behind in their rents. Many of the small farmers eventually sank into a chronic indebtedness from which they could not escape.

For most late-sixteenth-century working people, economic conditions in Essex towns were not better than in the countryside. Confronting the same inflationary pressures, well-to-do townspeople were trimming their staffs and making fewer purchases. It was difficult, as a result, for the unskilled laborers, porters, and servants to find work, and they also had to pay more for food and other necessities. Finally, there were also large numbers of vagrants and vagabonds who were tied neither to town nor country. They drifted from place to place, struggling to survive by working odd jobs, stealing from farms, or robbing fellow travelers.[27]

Against this already precarious backdrop came a series of truly miserable crop failures between 1594 and 1598. Meager harvests were not new to Essex. In fact, one poor yield every four years was probably typical in the late sixteenth century. However, the mid-1590s entailed not only severe but successive crop failures, and the result was especially disastrous because years of eroded purchasing power left most people without resources to cushion the impact. Marriage rates and birthrates declined, deaths increased, and there was widespread hunger.[28]

Rates of property crime also increased. Specifically, between 1559 and 1593, there were steady, but moderate, increases in rates of robbery, burglary, and theft in Essex. Then, concomitant with the series of harvest failures, property crime rates surged dramatically between 1594 and 1598. According to lawyer-turned-historian Joel Samaha, all signs suggest that hunger and desperation made ordinary people, not professional criminals, steal. Supporting this interpretation are a number of facts: most of those convicted were poor workers, and 85 percent of those found guilty were convicted of single rather than multiple offenses. Further, each year rates of crime were lowest at harvest time, when food was most plentiful.[29]

After 1598 there were better harvests, and economic circumstances began to take on normal appearances again. Rates of marriage picked up, but so too did rates of out-of-wedlock births. In fact, as we have previously described, they peaked during the first years of the seventeenth century. Why would the highest out-of-wedlock rates occur once recovery began? Keith Wrightson and David Levine propose that during the worst crisis years of the mid-1590s, young people knew that they could not afford to marry and set up independent households. Even the costs of a wedding gown or the meat and ale for guests at a wedding would have been prohibitive. Marriage, then, was simply out of the question so courtship, including premarital intercourse, was postponed.[30]

When recovery began, young people thought their marriage prospects were better than they really were, and courtship resumed. They underestimated how much the resources of their parents and of their potential employers had been depleted by years of adversity. The young people counted on jobs or dowries or help in getting established when they whispered commitments to each other and made love, but their expectations for the future could not be met. The woman's pregnancy could not act as a signal for them to marry, and out-of-wedlock births resulted. As economic conditions began to improve between 1600 and 1607, *at least* 50 percent of all nonmarital births were due to unexpectedly delayed marriages.[31]

Thus, two figures peaked simultaneously: the nonmarital birth-rate and the proportion of such births that were due to postponed marriages. There is no reason to assume that an increase in premarital sexual activity was an important precursor to this apex in out-of-wedlock births. Sexual activity probably was not higher in the early seventeenth century than it had been at most other times in the past (with the exception of just a few years in the mid-1590s). Premarital pregnancies likely continued to occur at the same rate as well. It is reasonable to conclude, therefore, that the dramatic increase in out-of-wedlock births at the turn of the seventeenth century did not rest upon changes in moral standards or in premarital behavior associated with those standards.

It also seems clear that there were no inducements to women (or men), from town or church, that could have made out-of-wedlock children seem desirable. We have noted that a daughter's pregnancy might make her father more generous in helping her to marry and set up an independent household. Perhaps some couples overestimated what the woman's father would be able to provide and intentionally sought the added leverage of her pregnancy. However, such miscalculations could not have contributed much to out-of-wedlock rates, given that nearly one half of the fathers of marrying couples had already died and many of those still living were known to have no resources.

THE AFTERMATH

It has been relatively easy to attribute the rapid increase in out-of-wedlock births to economically suppressed opportunities to marry, and not to inducements or changes in public morality. Explaining the post-1610 decline in nonmarital birthrates is much more complex, though. Even the figures themselves may be more suspect.

Let us begin with the basic facts, as we know them: the rate of decline in Terling's out-of-wedlock births was about as steep as the previous incline. By 1630 it had fallen from its peak of nearly 10 percent to about 3 percent, and by 1660 it was down to almost 1 percent—roughly what it had been in 1560.[32] This decline was accompanied by generally improved economic conditions. Courtship and marriage could again be more tightly connected, materially speaking. However, the social order in Essex was enduringly affected by the economic dislocations of the late sixteenth century. Of particular importance was a polarization of society that involved the growth of a lower class that was defined not only as poorer than the rest, but also as culturally different. As the overall rate fell, the proportion of nonmarital births coming from the lowest social groups in Terling increased. The mothers tended to be a mix of servants, women considered to be local whores, and vagabonds.

A series of early seventeenth-century Puritan ministers were successful in persuading the upper levels of Terling society to conform to the letter of Christian teaching with respect to nonmarital relations.[33] Punishments for those who deviated then became both more likely and more severe. For example, we previously noted that after 1610 there was a greater probability of an unmarried woman being rebuked once she was known to be pregnant. The women who actually bore out-of-wedlock children had always faced a greater risk of punishment, but as the seventeenth century progressed, they faced more severe condemnations. For example, during the 1620s and 1630s, unmarried Essex mothers were regularly sentenced to the house of correction (for three months) for repeat offenses. In the following decades, women were more likely to face three months of incarceration for a first offense, and the fathers of children born out of wedlock were increasingly likely to be whipped when they too came from the bottom of Terling's social hierarchy.[34] It was probably easier for the church and civic courts to impose punishments on men and women whose lower-class backgrounds made them morally suspect even before they were charged with anything.

In sum, during the seventeenth century there were growing disincentives for unmarried people in Terling to have children, and sentiments in most of the community increasingly condemned nonmarital sexual relations. Both of these trends corresponded with improving economic conditions. Because all occurred more or less together, it is very difficult to infer how much of the decline in out-of-wedlock births was due to each of these trends. Furthermore, we must conclude with a word of caution regarding the mid- and late-seventeenth-century figures. Many Essex ministers came to believe that baptism should be withheld from infants born out of wedlock even though this belief ran counter to community opinion. Some ministers continued to baptize all infants, and some did not.

Baptism records, as we have seen, are critical to historical reconstructions of nonmarital birthrates. A decline in baptisms of infants born out of wedlock could, therefore, be responsible for some spurious lowering of contemporary estimates of the rate. That rate almost certainly did decline after 1610, but perhaps by less than the figures imply. The conclusion that seems most secure is that excessive optimism after years of economic deterioration led to a steep increase in out-of-wedlock rates, and improved economic conditions as well as increased public condemnation and punishment—in some combination—then led to a reduction in rates, but perhaps by less than the figures imply.

NOTES

1. The labyrinth of underground rooms was built in 1953, but was not publicly disclosed until 1992. Jean Hawkes, "Officials' Underground Activities," *The Times Educational Supplement*, no. 4153, Feb. 2, 1996.

2. For further description of the Dutch immigrants in Colchester, see C. G. A. Clay, *Economic Expansion and Social Change, Vol II* (Cambridge:

Cambridge University Press, 1984), and Malcolm Thick, "Root Crops and the Feeding of London's Poor in the Late Sixteenth and Early Seventeenth Centuries," in John Chartres and David Hey (Eds.), *English Rural Society, 1500–1800* (Cambridge: Cambridge University Press, 1990).

3. For further description of the community, see Keith Wrightson, *English Society 1580–1680* (New Brunswick, NJ: Rutgers University Press, 1982).

4. Keith Wrightson and and David Levine, *Poverty and Piety in an English Village* (New York: Oxford University Press, 1995), pp. 80–81.

5. The preceding figures are taken from figure 5.1 in David Levine and Keith Wrightson, "The Social Context of Illegitimacy in Early Modern England," in Peter Laslett, Karla Oosterveen, and Richard M. Smith (Eds.), *Bastardy and Its Comparative History* (Cambridge, MA: Harvard University Press, 1980).

6. Ibid. (Figure 5.1). The preceding figures are all birth ratios. To calculate conventional nonmarital birthrates, we would need to know not only birth records, but also the marital status of all women in Terling. The latter information is not available. Therefore, the closest approximation is provided by calculating a nonmarital fertility rate. It is the ratio of nonmarital births to marriages per year. It often provides a crude but indicative picture of the overall rate. Between 1600 and 1610 this nonmarital fertility measure also increased markedly in Essex. See the discussion in chapter 3 in Peter Laslett, *Family Life and Illicit Love in Earlier Generations* (Cambridge: Cambridge University Press, 1977).

7. Terling had no permanent courts of its own, though. The closest village courts met in nearby Chelmsford (see figure 4.1), and difficult cases were often referred to courts in London. Most religious offenses were presented by Terling's churchwardens at the twice-yearly visits of the archdeacon of Colchester.

8. For further description of hiding and eliminating out-of-wedlock births, see Alan Macfarlane, "Illegitimacy and Illegitimates in English History," in Laslett, Oosterveen, and Smith, p. 77.

9. Wrightson and Levine, pp. 125–127, 132–133.

10. For further discussion of the alehouses and the increasing control over them during this period, see Wrightson.

11. Ibid.

12. For detailed examples of such exploitive relationships in the county of Somerset during the early seventeenth century, see G. R. Quaife, *Wanton Wenches and Wayward Wives* (New Brunswick, NJ: Rutgers University Press, 1979).

13. Wrightson and Levine. A similar pattern is described in Earls Colne, an Essex village about 10 miles north of Terling. See Macfarlane.

14. Wrightson and Levine, pp. 127–132.

15. And given the short life expectancies of the period, it was unusual for couples to celebrate more than a twentieth anniversary. See John R. Gillis, *For Better, for Worse* (New York: Oxford University Press, 1985).

16. See the discussion of social class and family formation in Wrightson.

17. Gillis, pp. 21–29

18. Quaife, pp. 39, 49.

19. When either party broke off a relationship that once seemed headed toward marriage, the gifts that had been given often became a matter of contention. Court records of the period are full of cases where individuals and families could not agree on whether gifts that had been given during courtship had to be returned once the betrothal was off. See Gillis.

20. See the discussion in Quaife, pp. 165–171.

21. For further discussion, see Macfarlane as well as Quaife.

22. Correspondingly, diaries from the time imply that decision making often involved give-and-take discussions between husbands and wives. Apparently there were also fewer cases of wife beating than the popular culture would suggest. See Wrightson.

23. Quaife p. 46. He also notes that pregnancy could give the bargaining male a good deal more leverage with his girlfriend's father, who could be expected to try to induce the man to marry his daughter in order to preserve family honor. Quaife, pp. 92–95.

24. Gillis, pp. 92–96.

25. For further discussion of seventeenth-century weddings, see ibid. and Wrightson.

26. Edward A. Wrigley and R. S. Schofield, *The Population History of England, 1541 to 1871* (Cambridge, MA: Harvard University Press, 1981). See figure 10.

27. Wrightson.

28. Essex was spared the terminal starvation that the series of ruinous harvests brought to other parts of England, though. See Andrew B. Appleby, *Famine in Tudor and Stuart England* (Stanford, CA: Stanford University Press, 1978).

29. Crimes of violence, by contrast, hardly fluctuated at all during this period. Detailed analyses of crime rates in Essex are provided by Joel Samaha, *Law and Order in Historical Perspective* (New York: Academic Press, 1974).

30. Wrightson and Levine.

31. This calculation assumes that none of the unclassified nonmarital births would be attributed to postponed marriages if more information were available. Figures are from Wrightson and Levine, pp. 130–134. As previously noted, throughout the entire period about one-third of all nonmarital births were attributable to unforeseen delays in marriage. See also Wrightson, pp. 190–191.

32. Ibid. Figure 5.1.

33. And when they did not conform, and pregnancies resulted, they were more likely to have the resources to hide out of wedlock births, for example, by temporarily moving away. However, the growing class difference in the seventeeth century appears primarily to be a reflection of different modes of conduct.

34. Many of the laws had been on the books for many years. What changed was the probability of enforcement and punishment. See Wrightson.

5

Madrid, Spain, 1760–1800

In 1572, near the center of Madrid, Spain, a small twelve-bed asylum that had been dedicated to caring for sick priests began also to take in abandoned infants. These newborns (whom the Spanish called, "*expositos*") were found outside the doors of churches and private dwellings, and on deserted street corners. In the following years, more infants were left right on the hospital's front steps, and it expanded and dedicated itself exclusively to the care of these infants. In 1615 the hospital (known as the "Inclusa") became one of the royal hospitals of Madrid, which symbolically placed the king in the role of surrogate father to the unfortunate *expositos*.[1]

The admissions records of the Inclusa are a major source of information about nonmarital births in Madrid during the later part of the eighteenth century. They are not a perfect source because, as we will see, it is difficult to be certain which of the admitted infants were officially fatherless and which were abandoned solely because their parents lacked the resources to care for them. In addition, the Inclusa did not receive all the infants born out of wedlock: some were not abandoned, others died of exposure or were eaten by dogs or wild pigs before they could be brought to the hospital, and still others were brought to different institutions that cared for *expositos*. Nevertheless, as the primary hospital for foundlings, the records of the Inclusa provide an extremely important barometer of nonmarital births in Madrid. These records suggest that there probably was a substantial increase in out-of-wedlock births at the end of the eighteenth century, and other sources of demographic data from the period also point in the same direction.

We will turn shortly to an examination of the Inclusa's records, and then to an analysis of other changes that were occurring at the time in Madrid and across Spain. We will try to identify the variables that may have been responsible for the increase in nonmarital births as reflected in admissions to the Inclusa. First, however, let us turn to a brief examination of the hospital itself and its physical setting in the Puerta del Sol, a bustling plaza in the center of Spain's capital.

THE INCLUSA AND PUERTA DEL SOL

In the Middle Ages, when Madrid was a walled city, Puerta del Sol was an entrance gate to the city at its eastern edge. With the later expansion of the city, the Puerta del Sol's location became more central, and it became a plaza, or square, where several radial streets converged, as il-

Figure 5.1
Puerta del Sol, Late Eighteenth Century

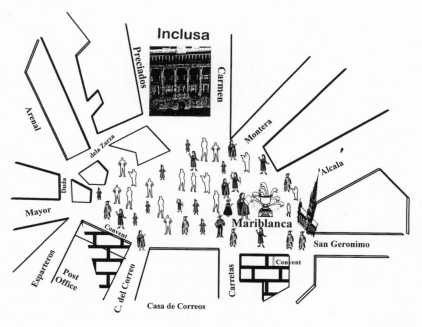

Source: From Charles E. Kany, *Life and Manners in Madrid* (New York: AMS Press, 1970), p. 53.

lustrated in figure 5.1. The city's activities were historically concentrated in such plazas, and Puerto del Sol became the most important of them after a new post office, which was also used to house a garrison of soldiers, was constructed on the square in 1768. (Today the same site houses the Ministry of the Interior.) This square was the political, economic, and intellectual center of the capital in the late eighteenth century and for decades thereafter. To most Spaniards as well as visitors, the Puerta del Sol provided the period's single most widely recognized icon of Madrid.

Near the center of the Puerta del Sol, and serving as one of its distinguishing landmarks in the eighteenth century, was a very ornate fountain called the Mariblanca. Hundreds of professional water carriers gathered daily under the fountain's spouts, and then competed with each other and with ordinary citizens, all of whom were trying simultaneously to fill their pitchers. Intricate rules governed one's order in the lines, but they were rarely enforced, and the pushing and shoving around the fountain helped to define the character of the entire plaza.

The crowded square teemed with itinerant gypsies and beggars, soldiers, shoppers, travelers, and vendors of all kinds. Country folks who journeyed to Madrid were cautioned about city ways, and the Puerta del Sol in particular. One publication providing advice to strangers, published in 1784, stated:

If anyone accosts you, saying, "Sir, would you like to . . . buy this ring I have found?," pay no attention . . . for it is worthless. . . . If you enter some church and see a man near you with hands uplifted in prayer . . . flee from him with greatest speed, for he is nothing but a pickpocket.[2]

Something or other was always happening to make the Puerta del Sol interesting. For example, it was a major stop along the route prisoners were taken when their punishment included public display. Seated on a mule, the prisoner was led through the streets with a town crier leading the way, announcing the prisoner's crime and punishment. The small procession began at the royal prison and entered Puerta del Sol from the west. It moved across the middle of the square to the Mariblanca, circled it and then exited. Among the social types that could always be found hanging around the square were young Spanish men called "dandies." These were men from well-to-do, but not aristocratic, backgrounds who most of all wanted to be fashionable. They were obsessed with the latest clothing and hair styles, manners of speaking, and other fads. After spending hours primping in front of their mirrors at home, many of the dandies spent some time each day hanging around the Puerta del Sol, hoping to be seen and admired while they were watching and discussing the well-dressed young women strolling through the plaza.[3]

The asylum that became the Inclusa was originally located just to the east of the square, on the calle (i.e., street) de San Jeronimo. When its activities as a foundling hospital expanded during the seventeenth century, it took over houses to the north of the square along calle del Carmen and calle de Preciados, finally concentrating on a small street between them. Like most of the buildings that surrounded it, the Inclusa was a brick building, four or five stories high, with few windows and a red tile roof. Its courtyard, with a small fountain, was open, and there were no obvious features to distinguish it from adjacent buildings. Most were of similar height, some had small balconies, and many contained steep staircases that ran from their top floors down to the filthy streets.[4]

The throngs of people that regularly assembled and moved through the Puerta del Sol provided the perfect setting for many of the mothers who used the services of the Inclusa. A young woman who had decided to abandon an infant could surreptitiously leave the baby at the open doorway of the Inclusa and then simply disappear into the crowds of the square. (There is some debate about whether this was a wrenching experience for women, running counter to their maternal instincts, or whether this was simply a good way for them to get rid of a problem.)[5]

The appointed administrator and the priests who ran the Inclusa were forced to operate it in a frugal manner. Especially when the infant rolls swelled but its budget remained flat, expenses had to be cut everywhere. The workloads of staff—nurses, laundresses, bookkeepers, and so forth—all increased. In noneconomic ways, however, the Inclusa's management was kindly paternalistic to its workforce. Employees and their relatives, for example, were often permitted to live in the hospital. Even among nonemployees, the Inclusa became an endearing institution to the working poor in Madrid by providing cash in return for various goods and services. Especially noteworthy in this respect were mothers nursing their own infants who were so desperate that they took money from the hospital to share their own baby's milk with an *exposito*. And as might be expected, there were frequent abuses, with horrific tales of *expositos* being tied up, tortured, and starved to death.[6]

EXPOSITOS AND NONMARITAL BIRTHS

Most of the infants admitted to the Inclusa during the seventeenth through the nineteenth centuries were abandoned by mothers (or parents) who were economically unable to provide for them. Many of the infants were also discarded to shield a woman and her family from the disgrace that would accompany a nonmarital birth if the birth were publicly acknowledged. And many of the abandoned infants were offspring of mothers who were both poor and unwed.

In traditional Spanish society, family honor was a central concern, and everyone was expected to uphold it. Where moral values were concerned, the appearance of virtue was at least as important as its practice, though. This placed a special emphasis upon acting correctly whenever one's actions or the consequences of those actions could be observed. Because Spain was dominated by patriarchal values, maintenance of family honor imposed special burdens upon women, who were required to follow a strict moral code: dress conservatively, act demurely, and be absolutely chaste. The most stigmatizing condition imaginable occurred when a woman had a child out of wedlock and this fact became known to people in the community.[7]

When nonmarital births increased at the close of the eighteenth century, there were a variety of institutional responses. For example, the queen financed a special room in the women's prison for pregnant inmates to give birth. Their babies were then brought to the Inclusa. The prison soon added two more delivery rooms to serve local women of higher status who were not inmates of the facility. The availability of these rooms and the high-quality medical services they offered were widely advertised in Madrid, but all arrangements were designed to ensure the mother's confidentiality. Thus even during the actual birthing process, women wore thick black veils to hide their faces. A week later they quietly returned to their homes, acting as if nothing had happened, and their newborns were brought to the Inclusa.[8]

The dictums of the Catholic Church also played a very important part in shaping the reactions to nonmarital births in Spain. The church, from the middle of the sixteenth century on, considered weddings officiated by a priest to be the only legitimate way a woman could be married. No woman who was not married in this way should, according to the church, be permitted to raise a child, because it would flaunt morality and improperly encourage people to be tolerant of sinful behavior.

Given these beliefs, the church insisted that the best way to handle out-of-wedlock births was to place the infants in the Inclusa. In addition, the Roman Catholic leadership was worried that, to avoid public shame, unmarried mothers would desert babies, who would die before they were baptized. The Inclusa, and foundling hospitals across Catholic Europe, were therefore designed also to assure that all abandoned infants were immediately baptized. Toward this end, the church also required that midwives receive clerical instruction so that they could perform the ceremony when newborns seemed in danger of dying before a priest could arrive.[9]

From many carefully preserved records it is possible to re-create, with some accuracy, statistical profiles of infant admissions to the Inclusa throughout the eighteenth century. Many of the residents of Madrid believed that virtually all of the admitted infants were officially fatherless and that they were abandoned for that reason. However, historian Joan Sherwood argues that after the first decades of the eighteenth century, the *expositos* were a mixed group. Using data that she was able to glean from the surprisingly well-preserved archives of the Inclusa regarding the admitted infants' parentage, name, age, and baptismal records, Sherwood estimates that between about 50 and 70 percent of the Inclusa's *expositos* were nonmarital births during the last half of the Eighteenth century. Her summary figures for the period are presented in table 5.1.

From the figures in table 5.1 we can see that for several decades immediately prior to 1780, the number of infants brought to the Inclusa varied across a relatively small range. This held true even though in some of those years there were large increases in Madrid's birthrate. (Thus,

Table 5.1
Expositos at the Inclusa, 1760–1800

Year	Total #	% Nonmarital	# Nonmarital
1760	692	50	343
1770	684	44	300
1780	748	50	374
1790	810	60	490
1795	1021	62	635
1800	1139	71	811

Source: From Joan Sherwood, *Poverty in Eighteenth-Century Spain* (Toronto: University of Toronto Press, 1988).

the size of the at-risk population was moving in the opposite direction.) After 1780, however—and especially between 1790 and 1800—there were unprecedented increases in the number of infants who were admitted and the number and percentage of them whose records suggested that they had been born out of wedlock. These increases in admissions occurred despite the fact there were steep declines in Madrid's overall birth rate during the 1790s.

As we consider what to make of Madrid's growing number of *expositos*, it should be noted that similar increases in the number of abandoned infants were recorded across much of Europe during this same time period. However, the percentage believed to be comprised of nonmarital births varied among nations and among cities within nations. A key variable seems to have been the degree to which either church officials or the administrators of foundling hospitals were willing to admit children whose parents were legally married but destitute. For example, in both Milan and Bologna, Italy, abandonments increased dramatically between 1770 and 1800. (Figures for these cities strongly resemble Madrid's.) In Bologna, where officials scrutinized admissions, the increase in abandoned infants consisted almost entirely of out-of-wedlock births. By contrast, in Milan, where babies could be left anonymously, the increase reflected both more nonmarital births and more births to married but impoverished parents.[10]

Finally, there is the question of how many of the infants left at Madrid's Inclusa were born to parents who were not from Madrid. There is no doubt that some came from the rural hinterlands. The poor from the countryside were attracted to Madrid's large soup kitchens (which served thousands per day around 1790) and the capital city's abundant supply of relatively cheap bread.[11] Many of these people moved periodically between Madrid and the countryside, depending upon whether the demand for unskilled labor was, at the time, greater in the city or its rural hinterland. Some of these migrating laborers would certainly have deposited unwanted infants at the Inclusa, and it seems appropriate to include their offspring in Madrid's tally because these people may reasonably be considered part of the extended population of the capital area.

It is likely that the Inclusa's records were not seriously inflated by infants born to mothers who were not from the Madrid area. Few persons from outside the Madrid region would have utilized the Inclusa in the eighteenth century because the city was not easily accessed. Unlike most European capitals, it lacked water-based routes, so traveling to Madrid meant strenuous walking or riding on horseback.[12] Few parents would have tried to reach Madrid's Inclusa from any distance, therefore, and had they tried, it is doubtful that many of their newborn infants would have survived the ordeal.

In sum, despite some known errors in the figures from the Inclusa, we can reasonably conclude that they validly reflect a substantial increase in nonmarital births in Madrid in the closing decades of the eighteenth century. We turn now to theories about why this increase occurred. Some explanations view economic crises, due to crop failures and inflation, as preventing couples from marrying and forming households when women became pregnant. Other explanations point to normative changes associated with urban life in Madrid as having led to a breakdown in traditional morality, with nonmarital births as one indicator of the social and moral disintegration. In the following pages, we will review the evidence pertaining to economic downturns, normative changes, and the two in combination.

MADRID'S GROWTH AND CHANGE

Madrid grew rapidly during the 1700s, from about 25,000 people at the start of the century to perhaps 175,000 by its close.[13] There was some natural increase, due to an excess of births over deaths. Most of the increase in population, however, was the result of migration from other Spanish cities and from the countryside surrounding Madrid, in which people in small communities grew wheat, grapes, and olives and raised sheep.

There were three traditional groups of agricultural workers. The best off were peasants who owned their own fields or livestock. A second group rented land from well-to-do peasants or absentee landlords and paid cash or in-kind rents. The poorest group were laborers who hired on for seasonal work in olive plantations or on agricultural estates. They were described in stark terms: "Nearly naked and with only the ground for a bed, they . . . live on . . . bread and soup . . . but when bad weather stops work . . . starving, homeless, and hopeless, they are forced to beg."[14]

During the first half of the eighteenth century, there were small streams of migrants to Madrid that were primarily comprised of people trying to escape from hopeless poverty. Included here were the wives and children of the seasonal laborers, for whom the countryside offered no work. In Madrid they hoped to be employed as servants and maids or else receive support from one of the city's numerous charitable associations. Mostly young and unmarried immigrants from the slums of

Sevilla, Valencia, and other Spanish cities also settled in Madrid, and formed concentrated enclaves. In the middle of the eighteenth century, their quarters of the city offered rich street life that sometimes flaunted Spain's traditional standards. On May Day, for example, the young people selected the most beautiful young woman to be the May queen. Playing tambourines and guitars, neighbors and friends formed a procession and carried her through the streets to a specially constructed throne. The participants solicited money from spectators and used their contributions to buy food and drink for a public festival that was considered wild by traditionalists. The party atmosphere and the women's flamboyant actions and their bright shawls and sparkling jewelry made them stand out, and they attracted the attention of Madrid's dandies, who were more than a little interested in joining their parties. However, the women's boyfriends posed definite risks to any of the dandies who were intrigued enough to follow the women too far into the women's own neighborhoods.[15]

The lower-class women whose colorful dress and brazen actions enticed the dandies were a social type collectively referred to as *maja*. While traditional women in Madrid left their homes wearing black cloaks and ignored people to whom they had not been properly introduced, the *maja* and women influenced by this social type would wear red shawls and flirt with strangers. Their male counterparts were *majo*: brazen, cigar-smoking men, colorfully dressed, always ready to fight.[16]

The *maja* image was powerful in the last half of the eighteenth century in Madrid. For many upper-class women, it was a social type to be emulated, at least at selective times. One young lady of society explained that the maja's sexy air of effrontery was her model: "All I cared for was to copy in my actions that arrogance, insolence, vanity and boldness. . . . I was determined to acquire that air at any price."[17] To properly appreciate how much the *maja* image challenged Spain's traditions, realize that the social repression of the Spanish Inquisition, headquartered in Madrid, still had some real power. Although few women were still burned at the stake, the Inquisition's last victim was burned in 1780.

For the poor peasant girls who lived in the country, stories about eighteenth-century Madrid were enticing because, like cities everywhere, Madrid promised freedom and opportunity. The opportunity tended to be limited to the difficult work of a servant or maid, which entailed a long day of cleaning, sewing, cooking, shaving a master's face, and fixing a mistress's hair. The pay was meager, but it was more than peasant girls could earn outside of the capital. The freedom and excitement that beckoned many of the young women to Madrid were limited by work-related constraints, but again, there was more opportunity for fun than they would have found back on the farm. When the country girls who had worked as maids in Madrid returned home, permanently or for visits, they espoused lifestyles that seemed scandalous to the locals. One country priest, in 1784, summarized how his parishioners viewed Madrid's effect upon the typical young woman by stating, "It has become proverbial to say: she has been a maid in town, and that says it all."[18]

Many of the naive young women who came to Madrid from the countryside were poorly prepared for city life, and were easily robbed, conned, and lured into sexual relations. When they became pregnant, their boyfriends often disappeared, and young unmarried mothers found themselves with few choices for their infants other than the Inclusa. While working as maids, a number of young women were also seduced by their masters, and when they became pregnant they were paid off to go away. They moved on, then, and many deposited their infants at the Inclusa on their way.

During the second half of the eighteenth century, Madrid continued to attract the poor from the countryside, but there were even more of them coming. As a result of several prolonged periods of extraordinarily harsh weather and poor harvests over the last third of the century, seasonal laborers found work more scarce. Simultaneous with reduced crop output, population growth in Madrid led to increased demand for foodstuffs. Land values inflated as a result, and many of the middle-level peasants were unable to maintain leases to land their families had been farming for generations. In response to the widespread suffering in rural areas, the government began to sell idle farmland on the open market. The objective of the plan was to increase total crop production, and it was partly successful, but the program obviously did nothing to help the growing numbers of poor peasants who could not afford to buy land at any price. As they were pushed off the land, they were pulled to Madrid in the belief they would find better opportunities there.[19]

In the 1760s, hunger was also widespread among Madrid's poor, and it led to street riots. Because government officials feared that urban unrest could lead to political upheaval, they responded by making sure that adequate food reached the capital and further, by subsidizing the cost of basic foodstuffs. There were still periodically severe food shortages in Madrid during the following decades. However, the magnitude of the deprivation was even worse in the countryside, and this continued to encourage peasants to migrate to the city.

As Madrid became larger and more diverse during the late eighteenth century, it also became more cosmopolitan, influenced by more liberal European ideas, particularly from Italy and France. Among the rich, travel between Madrid and Paris increased, and books and plays from Paris, Rome, and Turin were "smuggled" into Madrid, offering those who could afford it a glimpse of the latest trends in fashion, politics, and courtship—and as a result, customs changed. For example, among the upper classes in Spain there was a long tradition of male friends serving as close confidants and escorts of married women. Although the men in these relationships frequently praised the women's beauty, such compliments were not considered flirtatious, and almost all of these relationships had traditionally been platonic. During the last half of the eighteenth century, however, these liaisons increasingly provided a context in which there were extramarital sexual relations.[20]

Wealthier Spaniards from the countryside and from other Spanish cities were also attracted to Madrid during this period, because it came to symbolize exciting lifestyles that could not be pursued elsewhere. In one popular play of 1772, for example, a newly rich peasant tells his wife that because he has often traveled to Madrid, he "knows the ways of the world." He tries to convey this to her by presenting some examples of how social life has changed, but is frustrated by her apparent slowness in grasping the idea. Finally he asks her to imagine that they were not married and had just met. How would she respond if he told her how beautiful she was? She said she would blush and tell him how shameless he was to say such a thing. He replied that in Madrid he would treat her reaction as a joke, and take hold of her by her hands. Shocked at the thought of such boldness, she exclaimed that she would hit him over the head with a chair if he tried to do that. "There you go!" he complained again, in exasperation. "That's just what a woman would do here in the country . . . but in Madrid that would not do at all."[21]

EXPLAINING INCREASED NONMARITAL BIRTHS

To some degree the increase in the number of out-of-wedlock births in late-eighteenth-century Madrid was due to a change in values that might even be considered a sexual revolution. This explanation would certainly fit the increase in nonmarital sexual activity that apparently occurred in upper-class circles. In fact, as we saw, it was precisely Madrid's relative sexual freedom that was a major attraction to upper-status groups outside the city. However, it is likely that this group made a relatively small contribution to the overall increase in the known number of nonmarital births, especially when admissions to the Inclusa serve as the index. Upper-class women ordinarily had the resources with which to hide births that would officially be considered out-of-wedlock (if they were known) and thereby maintain family honor.

The relative permissiveness of Madrid's extramarital norms also contributed to the increasing nonmarital birth rate among the poor young people from the countryside who were swarming into the city. However, it is not clear how much of the increase to attribute to more permissive norms per se, because the lives of these young immigrants were also simultaneously impacted by severely deteriorating economic conditions. As a result, it is not clear how much may have been due to a change in values; many lower-class couples undoubtedly found themselves unable to follow Spanish marital customs no matter how much they might have wanted to do so. To illustrate, the traditional value that had been placed upon a woman's sexual purity probably was insufficient to hold back those women who saw prostitution as the only paying work available to them. Families were certainly mortified by such behavior, and no one would be happy to undergo this self-inflicted shame, but what if starvation was the only alternative? To illustrate further, marriage as soon as a woman's pregnancy was known could have remained a cultural ideal, but couples who could not afford to establish a household may have been unable to comply with the ideal when the woman became pregnant. Thus they may have felt they had little choice but remain unmarried and place the child born out of wedlock in the Inclusa. In sum, the behavior of people of very limited means did not necessarily reflect their values.

In many respects the poor young migrants to Madrid can readily be viewed as an example of what Ephraim Mizruchi calls "surplus populations." They are the product of an imbalance that is created when the population of a place increases relative to the number of organizational or institutional positions that are available. Historically, such groups have been created when religious associations are too successful in recruiting people to monastic ways of life, when unemployment reaches high levels during severe depressions, and when rural migrants stream into urban areas that are not economically expanding, such as Madrid in the late 1700s. Because there are no positions for these people, they have no social place: they are not under the control of the organizations and institutions that could otherwise help to maintain social conventions. They frequently lack commitment to the status quo, therefore, and tend to engage in deviant and protest behaviors, which are viewed as threatening to the traditional norms of their societies.[22]

The rootless young people in Madrid were a surplus population for whom positions that would tie them to the social order did not exist. Their high rate of nonmarital births was only one of several ways in which their weak compliance with traditional norms was expressed. They were also apparently guilty of engaging in high rates of robbery, assault, and other criminal actions. As in the case of Essex two hundred years earlier, discussed in the last chapter, we again see nonmarital births constituting an element of a complex of deviant behaviors.

However, Joan Sherwood also presents a persuasive case for the importance of poverty as constraining people's ability to marry, regardless of their values. From her detailed analysis of Inclusa records, she shows that after 1770 various admissions figures increasingly deviated from the birth patterns of the city as a whole. For example, prior to about 1770, rates of admission to the Inclusa, by month, were similar to all monthly birth rates in the city. In the closing decades of the eighteenth century, however, admission rates ran counter to overall births, peaking in the winter months. The significance of this seasonal peak in admissions is that it occurred, each year, just before new crops would be harvested, bringing down food prices, at least temporarily. This reflects a "hardship pattern," Sherwood concludes, in which poverty most prevented marriage when food prices were high, and so, out-of-wedlock births were highest when food prices were highest. This was, it will be recalled, the pattern in the county of Essex as well. In addition, Sherwood reports that after 1790 birthrates in Madrid fell but the number of admissions to the Inclusa increased, the latter a function of increasingly widespread poverty in the area surrounding Madrid.[23]

Theoretically, it is also possible to speculate that, over time, economic constraints and people's values came to prompt increasingly similar ways of behaving. While we often think about people's values as preceding their conduct, the reverse may also be true in the long run. Put in other words, values may change in response to repeated behavior, as people come to value what they have to do anyway. This is a corollary of the old "sour grapes" argument: "those grapes would not have tasted good even if I had been able to get them." Thus the prolonged adversity may have led poor young people to downplay the desirability of marriage, given that it seemed unattainable, and this devaluing may have been especially pronounced among "the rootless who had no stake in preserving traditional patterns."[24]

THE AWFUL AFTERMATH

In the first decades of the nineteenth century, rates of admission to the Inclusa remained very high, sometimes eclipsing the previous peak rate of 1800. The percentage of admitted infants that was born out of wedlock stayed about the same, but as the sheer number of infants being remanded to the Inclusa increased, so too did the absolute number whose mothers were not married.[25]

The increase in the number of foundlings had multiple causes. Economic difficulties persisted, and there were also wars and social turmoil. Napoleon had come to power and conquered much of Europe. In 1807 Spain signed a treaty permitting French occupation, and thousands of French soldiers moved into Madrid. The Spanish government was both corrupt and inefficient, and when the country was also hit by plagues and bad harvests, it was no longer able to respond. Civil unrest grew, and one year after the French became an occupying force, a riot broke out in the Puerta del Sol, leading to a war of liberation. It was also a civil war, with Spaniards on different sides, and fighting continued for several years.

Our analysis in this chapter ended with the year 1800 because external changes made circumstances in the following decades non-comparable. Most notable was the fact that the thousands of French soldiers occupying Madrid were at least partly responsible for the increase in the number of nonmarital births that occurred early in the nineteenth century.

Meanwhile, the resources of the Inclusa were strained beyond the bursting point, and in the turmoil and fighting, too few people noticed what was happening to the infants. There was not enough milk, the dedicated but inadequate staff had too little expertise, and crowded conditions exacerbated epidemics within the nursery. The survival of foundlings was always problematic in the Inclusa because some of them were injured during birth and others were malnourished or ill before their admission, but their survival rates became dramatically worse. Between 1760 and 1799, the ratio of admissions to deaths within the hospital was always more than two to one, and it often exceeded three to one. Between 1800 and 1812, however, mortality among the infants soared. The ratio of admissions to deaths fell to roughly three to two. In the worst years, infant death rates exceeded 85 percent.[26] In Spain's turmoil, the *expositos* of the Inclusa were truly the victims.

NOTES

1. In modern times, under government auspices, but at a different site, the institution has evolved into a pediatric hospital. For further discussion of the Inclusa, see Joan Sherwood, *Poverty in Eighteenth-Century Spain* (Toronto: University of Toronto Press, 1988).

2. Charles E. Kany, *Life and Manners in Madrid* (New York: AMS Press, 1970) p. 59.

3. For further discussion of the dandies, see Carmen M. Gaite, *Love Customs in Eighteenth-Century Spain* (Berkeley, CA: University of California Press, 1991), pp. 44–54.

4. This description is taken from Sherwood and from Kany.

5. For further discussion of maternal instincts, see Edward Shorter, *The Making of the Modern Family* (New York: Basic Books, 1977), and David I. Kertzer, *Sacrificed for Honor* (Boston: Beacon Press, 1993).

6. See Sherwood, especially chapter 4.

7. For further discussion of family honor, from a male point of view, see Jesus Cruz, *Gentlemen, Bourgeois, and Revolutionaries* (Cambridge: Cambridge University Press, 1996). From a female perspective, see the essays in Magdalena S. Sanchez and Alain Saint-Saens (Eds.), *Spanish Women in the Golden Age* (Westport, CT: Greenwood Press, 1996).

8. Sherwood, p. 109.

9. For further discussion of abandonment and the role of the Catholic Church in Europe, see Kertzer.

10. For further information about the Italian cities, see Kertzer.

11. Sherwood, p. 120.

12. Cruz, p. 34.

13. For several estimates and discussion of their accuracy, see Richard Herr, *Rural Change and Royal Finances in Spain* (Berkeley, CA: University of California Press, 1989), especially Appendix A.

14. Quoted in Richard Herr, *The Eighteenth-Century Revolution in Spain,* (Princeton, NJ: Princeton University Press, 1958), p. 105.

15. Kany, pp. 220–221.

16. Visual images of *maja* and *majo* types are depicted in numerous Goya sketches drawn in the late 1770s. See, for example, the text and reproductions in F. D. Klingender, *Goya in the Democratic Tradition* (New York: Schocken Books, 1968); and Anthony Hull, *Goya: Man among Kings* (New York: Hamilton Press, 1987).

17. Quoted in Gaite, p. 68.

18. Quoted in Ibid., p. 61.

19. See Herr, *Rural Change*, and Cruz.

20. See Gaite.

21. Quoted in Kany, p. 215.

22. Ephraim H. Mizruchi, *Regulating Society* (New York: Free Press, 1983).

23. Sherwood, pp. 116–118.

24. Ibid., p. 123.

25. For nineteenth-century figures, see Florentina Y Benicia Vidal Galache, *Bordes Y Bastardos* (Madrid: Literaria Compania, 1995).

26. See Sherwood, chapter 6, and Vidal Galache.

6

Jamaica, West Indies, 1950–1985

Most Americans think first about Jamaica as a resort. It is a popular winter vacation site for Americans because it is less than 600 air miles south of Miami, and it offers warm weather and beautiful Caribbean beaches. That is an accurate picture of only a small part of the island, though. Many of its flat coastal plains have historically contained vast sugar plantations, formerly worked by slaves brought from Africa to the West Indies. Much of the island's interior, in marked contrast, is rugged and mountainous, and has much cooler temperatures. These interior regions are devoted to mining and a few specialized export crops. Especially notable is the fine coffee which is exported to the United States, Canada, and England. It is primarily grown in the Blue Mountains, a range located at the eastern edge of the island. There are also sizable foreign markets for the cannabis that is illegally cultivated at dozens of sites on the island.

In order to provide an overview of Jamaica and to identify the location of specific places that will be discussed in parts of this chapter, a map of the island is presented in figure 6.1.

THE ISLAND'S BACKGROUND

It was in 1492, after his third voyage to the New World, that Columbus and his men first landed in Jamaica. The island's fertile plains attracted the Spaniards who brought orange trees and sugar cane to the island along with cattle and pigs. Spanish rulers proceeded to use Ja-

Figure 6.1
Jamaica

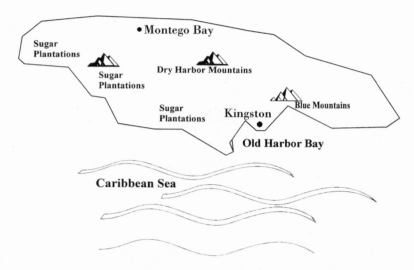

maica as a supply base, employing native Indian people—and later, Spanish settlers also—to provide food to support their military activities in Florida, Cuba, and Mexico. Epidemics kept down the size of colonial settlements on the island, but it remained an important supply base for the Spaniards until a large British naval force invaded in 1655. Jamaica remained more or less under British domination for most of the next three hundred years, though actual control over the island was contested, first by the Spanish, later by the French, still later by pirates, and most recently by the United States.[1]

The total land area of Jamaica is about the size of the state of Connecticut. Its population, overwhelmingly African in origin, increased between 1950 and 1985 from about 1.5 million persons to slightly over 2 million. The island's capital, Kingston (called "town" to distinguish it from "country"), contained between about one-fourth and one-third of the island's population during this period. Unlike the sparsely populated country, it is densely populated, with shantytown housing and rum shops featuring loud jukeboxes and all-night domino games. The city's hot, dusty, and crowded streets are shared by pedestrians, automobiles, goats, and public buses. These buses, packed with sweaty passengers, take commuters and visitors on potholed roads out of Kingston to dozens of small coastal and mountain villages.

Both town and country are poor. The nation's economic development has been slow, and the need to import items—from automobiles to milk and grain—has resulted in a growing foreign debt. Throughout most of the time period in question the official unemployment rate hovered around 20 percent which is very high, but it would be still higher if it took into account the large number of people who had only part-time or seasonal work as gardeners, maids, farm laborers, and the like. Precise figures are not available, but throughout the years in question (i.e., 1950 to 1985) employment prospects were especially bleak for young persons first entering the job market. Agricultural employment fell throughout the twentieth century, primarily because Jamaica's share of the world's sugar market declined. Manufacturing, tourism, and other sectors did not expand nearly enough to offset the agricultural constriction. As a result, the Jamaican economy was able to absorb no more than 20 percent of all of the island's new job seekers. This left a massive pool of young people completely shut out of the mainstream job market.[2]

Class and color in Jamaica have been historically linked since slavery was instituted in the seventeenth century. There is a very small upper class comprised of the families of corporate heads and large landowners. Almost all of these people are publicly considered to be white, even though some have African ancestry. The larger, but still small, middle class contains professionals, people who work in sales and own small stores. Their typical skin hue (or "complexion," according to the Jamaican's vocabulary) is socially identified as "brown." Most are persons of conspicuously mixed black and white or East Asian backgrounds. Finally, virtually all of the unskilled laborers, service workers, and unemployed persons in Jamaica's very large working and lower classes tend to be identified as black.

Even though the Jamaican population is overwhelmingly African in origin, in a mate most Jamaicans seem to favor "bright" (i.e., white or light-color) skin, "good" (i.e., straight) hair, narrow noses, and other white features. And the Jamaican women who are successful fashion models or win beauty contests tend to have a white appearance. It is important to remember that for ordinary Jamaicans, white skin implies both physical attractiveness and high status. An interesting illustration is provided by historian Laurie Gunst, who in 1984 overheard two elderly black women at a Kingston bus stop. The two were discussing an automobile accident that had just killed a young white couple from a wealthy family. "What a sad ting, eh?" one of the women said. "An' the two o' dem so nice an' white!"[3]

Birthrates on the island have been sufficiently high to result in modest growth, but further population increases have been offset by substantial out-migration of Jamaicans to the United States and Canada. The statistic that may most distinguish Jamaica among demographers, however, is its extremely high out-of-wedlock birth ratio: for well over one hundred years, the island's ratio of non-marital to all births has been among the very highest in the world. Presented in table 6.1 are out-of-wedlock ratios beginning with the earliest year in which data were recorded (1878), with greater detail for the years of maximum interest to us.

From table 6.1 we can see that the 1940s was the only decade during which there was any decline in out-of-wedlock ratios. These reductions were probably due to a "mass marriage movement" orchestrated by the (then) governor's wife.[4] She advocated child rearing within traditional marriages, and with support from public figures, she swayed sentiment in that direction for a brief time. The movement did not endure beyond her husband's term; however, given the way that nonmarital births have predominated in Jamaica, any decline in the proportion of such births is notable. We must simultaneously acknowledge that it was a very small decline, though, and that the ratio remained very high on an absolute

Table 6.1
Out-of-Wedlock Ratios in Jamaica, 1878–1984

Year	Ratio (% of All Births)	Year	Ratio (% of All Births)	Year	Ratio (% of All Births)
1878	59	1951	70	1969	76
1900	63	1954	72	1972	78
1921	70	1957	72	1975	78
1942	70	1960	72	1978	81
1945	69	1963	74	1981	83
1948	68	1966	75	1984	84

Source: Data through 1963 from Shirley F. Hartley, "Illegitimacy in Jamaica," in Peter Laslett, Karla Oosterveen, and Richard M. Smith (Eds.), *Bastardy and Its Comparative History* (Cambridge, MA: Harvard University Press, 1980), p. 387; 1966–1975 data are from Jamaica Department of Statistics, *Statistical Abstract* (Kingston: Department of Statistics, various years); 1978–1984 data are from United Nations, *1986 Demographic Yearbook* (New York: United Nations, 1986).

basis. After about 1950, the long-term trend toward higher ratios resumed.

The figures in table 6.1 are *ratios*, which calculate births to unmarried mothers as a percentage of all births. The same overall trend characterized the *rate* with which unmarried women gave birth; that is, the number of females who became mothers for every 1,000 unmarried women. Specifically, between the 1940s and the 1980s, that rate approximately doubled, from just over 100 women per 1,000 women to more than 200 women for each 1,000 who were unmarried.

Our detailed analysis of nonmarital births in Jamaica begins around 1950, following the slight decline observed during the 1940s, and examines the island over the next thirty-five years. We begin with an overview of Jamaican culture and social organization. We will follow this with an analysis of the features of Jamaican society that seem to be the most important correlates of the island's extremely high incidence of nonmarital births. Then we will focus upon variations within the island, that is, differences among its rural communities and city neighborhoods, in an effort to identify more precisely what accounts for high out-of-wedlock ratios and rates in Jamaica.

SLAVERY'S LEGACY

Between the late seventeenth century and the early nineteenth century, a few hundred thousand Africans were brought to Jamaica by slave traders and sold. Today their descendants comprise the core of the island, and their high ratios of out-of-wedlock births are attributed, by some analysts, to the legacy of slavery's restrictions upon their marriage and family formation. For example, concentrated numbers of African slaves worked on the island's sugar plantations, where their lives were governed by planter assemblies. According to the planters' legal codes, the blacks were explicitly the property of their white, British owners, and most of them treated their slaves more like property than people. As described by Orlando Patterson, this entailed isolating the slaves from their social and cultural heritage: taking away their African names and native religions and denying them basic rights to marry and raise children.[5]

After 1733, slaves in Jamaica were, according to law, to be sold individually unless they were parts of a family, in which case they were supposed to be sold as a family unit. However, this requirement was rarely enforced, and married black men and women were routinely sold separately, irrespective of the consequences of such sales upon slave families. Further, slave women could almost always be forced to provide sexual services for their owners. If the woman was married (and her union could only be to a black male), she was—on paper—protected from having to engage in sexual relations with her owner, but this law was not enforced either. Meanwhile, slave women were encouraged to have many children, especially after about 1780, as the British settlers began to fear abolition of the slave trade. Once she gave birth to six children, for example, a slave was excused from hard labor and her owner was exempt from paying taxes on her. These advantages accrued both to the slave and to her owner regardless of who fathered any of her children. Hence Jamaican slavery involved a situation in which marriage bonds could not mean very much to a black woman (or man), at the same time that strong inducements were offered to black women to have many children.6

No one can realistically ignore the lingering effects of slavery when trying to explain the distinctive marriage and birth patterns in Jamaica and other Caribbean nations. What is debatable, however, is how *much* to attribute to this slave legacy. Those who are concerned about exaggerating its importance feel that historical explanations of this type leave unanswered the important question of how some patterns instituted under slavery persist while others do not. Thus, some food dishes, hairstyles, and ways of dressing and speaking continued relatively unchanged on the island; but others underwent modification, and still others disappeared, temporarily or permanently. Therefore, with respect to out-of-wedlock births, we wish to know what it is about contemporary Jamaican social organization that accounts for the continuation of the high ratios.

Legacy-of-slavery explanations also tend implicitly to present too passive a view of black Jamaicans. As slaves they obviously had little power and few resources, but even on plantations they had some resources, and they used them creatively.7 To illustrate, female slaves were certainly exploited sexually, but many also used their masters' sexual attraction to serve their own ends. And where they could, the women worked together. The moment a master died, for example, his closest slave woman, with help from her female friends, would frequently abscond with as much of his money, clothing, and furniture as each could carry. In the eyes of the slaves, this was perfectly legitimate behavior. As one island proverb put it: "Thief from thief Massa God laugh."8 The point is that Jamaicans, like people everywhere, do not simply act in accordance with the strictures others try to impose. They also actively create their own patterns of behavior.

A final argument against viewing slavery as substantially explaining contemporary nonmarital birth patterns in Jamaica is the increase that occurred in both rates and ratios between 1950 and 1985 (see table 6.1.) Over one hundred years after emancipation in Jamaica, why attribute an increase of roughly 20 percent in the island's out-of-wedlock ratio to a legacy of slavery rather than to contemporary social forces?[9]

CULTURAL FEATURES AND NONMARITAL BIRTHS

Sexual Beliefs and Practices

Jamaicans by and large believe that people have very powerful sex drives. Attempts to deny the drive's expression through sexual intercourse risk illness or injury. To illustrate, if a man does not have enough sexual "discharge," toxins are believed to build up inside him and cause back problems. A Jamaican man experiencing back pains may therefore assume that the underlying cause of his problem is too little sexual intercourse. If a woman does not have enough sexual gratification, many Jamaicans contend, it can eventually cause her to become insane. Thus, for women, strange behavior and sexual abstinence are linked in people's minds. During courtship a young male trying to seduce his girlfriend will sometimes use these beliefs to try to scare her, warning the girl that she risks madness if she insist upon resisting his sexual advances.[10]

Attitudes toward women's premarital (and extramarital) sexual relations may, for several reasons, have more permissive aspects in the upper than the lower classes on the island. Knowledge of and utilization of contraceptives probably enabled upper-class couples to avoid unwanted pregnancies better than their counterparts in the lower class, who very infrequently used any means of birth control during the time in question. In addition, upper-class people were, overall, more likely to marry by any given age and more likely to view sexual relations as a normal precursor to marriage. However, their "lenient" attitudes were strictly confined to men and women of the same class and color.[11]

Because of their fear that females will be left alone and pregnant, lower-class parents and other kin tend to urge unmarried females to avoid nonmarital sexual relations. There is a double standard in this regard, because men are not warned. Older relatives caution girls to be wary of a male's tricks; to distrust men because they can be expected to promise a female everything to entice her to engage in sexual inter-course, but afterwards they will not deliver. A lot of the music played in Jamaica's many dance halls follows this theme. In the popular parable of Devon and Sharon, for example, the man tells Sharon that he owns a house, land, and a car. He says that he wants to make love to her and swears he will take care of her. However, she finds out he is a liar with no possessions, and she dumps him.[12]

From a survey of lower-class women conducted during the mid-1950s, sociologist Judith Blake reported that despite admonitions to stay away from males, about one-half of her respondents had engaged in sexual intercourse before age 17. Further, regardless of their age, very few of the respondents' first experiences involved a male with whom they had an enduring relationship.[13] In the late 1970s, anthropologist A. Lynn Bolles examined a sample of working-class women and found patterns much like Blake's, despite the twenty-year interval and differ-ences in the ways they selected their samples. Specifically, Bolles re-ported that about 25 percent of her respondents became unwed mothers before they reached aged 16 and that almost none of them had later contact with the male who fathered their firstborn child.[14]

Many of the women in Blake's sample recalled their initial sexual ex-periences as involving pressure from males to engage in acts they poorly understood at the time. (Their parents had tried to be strict, but had not provided much sex education.) For a majority of the girls who entered sexual unions by age 14 or 15, their first male partners were a good deal older. Blake did not obtain systematic data on age differences, but over one-half of the males who were the initial partners of these young girls were at least 5 years older; and a substantial number were 15 or more years older.

Some of the older men who consorted with young girls were itiner-ants who happened to live nearby and took advantage of their proximity. One young woman recalled:

Me and him were living close to each other . . . and while grandmother gone to market on Saturdays he . . . come to the house and ask me to friend him. . . .You know when you are a child you don't know what to say to a big man.[15]

However, many of the older men were stable members of the com-munity, and as the age difference between them and the girls they intro-duced to sex might imply, they had higher status and more power than their partners. Among these men were: foremen on plantations where the girls' families worked, sons of deacons where they went to church, landlords where they lived, and so on. The status and age differences provide at least circumstantial evidence that, for the youngest girls, entry into sexual relations may not have been entirely consensual.

Jamaican women rarely sought abortions, regardless of the circumstances in which they became pregnant. Moral repugnance to abortion is part of the reason. Furthermore, aspects of Jamaican culture provide strong counter-encouragements, even if the birth would be ill timed. For the female, childbirth is an affirmation of her status as an adult, and it demonstrates to all that she is healthy and fertile (not a barren "mule")—and these are very important considerations on the island. For the male, even if he does not intend to marry the woman, fathering a child is also desirable because it is viewed as "cementing" a woman: tying her to the man because she and the child will be dependent upon him for support. In the male view, this will make her more likely to be faithful to him in the future. Therefore, men tend to regard with distrust women that do not want to have children. As one man explained," Those women are worthless—want to run up and down, want to have no worry with children. I say it don't good at all. . . . Them women . . . a whore, them worthless, only looking money."[16]

Pregnancies rarely resulted in marriage, Blake reported, especially among very young girls. When the males who fathered their children were itinerants, a girl's pregnancy was a signal to move on and thus avoid any sanctions in the local community. Chasing after the men would not ordinarily have been fruitful anyway, because most of them lacked the financial resources to support their offspring. The fathers who were established men in the same community as the mother sometimes acknowledged paternity and provided support; but more typically they denied any involvement with the female, and given the insulation provided by their high status, the mother and her family then had little recourse but to raise the child themselves.

Nurture Kinship

Across the time period in question, that is, 1950 to 1985, an average of about 25 percent of all the births on the island were the offspring of a married couple living together. A roughly comparable number were born to unmarried couples who were living together prior to the birth. Some of these cohabitating couples later married, but many did not, and a significant proportion of those who did marry, before or after the birth, did not stay married. As a net result, very few Jamaican children lived with both of their biological parents.

In the period in question (as well as the present time) many infants' first homes were with their maternal grandmothers or other maternal kin, until their mothers could establish a separate household. This typically included her then-current boyfriend, who might or might not have been the child's father, and he might also have brought to the household children from one of his former relationships. If the child's mother and this man later decided to go their separate ways, the child could stay with either, or go to kin of either, though it has been most common for a child to remain with his or her mother. Whoever the child remained with was likely eventually to begin a relationship with someone new, and the child would then become part of another reconstituted family. Fortunately, and probably not accidentally, many features of the island's family system have made it relatively easy to assimilate newcomers into combined families.[17]

Terms of relationship in Jamaica reflect the fact that the social and biological dimensions of parenthood often do not coincide. More than in most cultures, Jamaicans readily distinguish between people who initially propagated children and those who currently nurture them. To illustrate, a "babymother" or a "babyfather" refers to a biological parent who is no longer closely involved in raising a child. An "acting father" or an "acting mother" refers to an adult who is not a child's biological parent but is currently living with someone who is a biological parent of the child's.

The above terms can imply a very strong distinction between the biological and the social whenthey are seen through the lens of American culture. However, to the people of Jamaica, the acting mother who cares for a child in her household can claim motherhood status almost the same as that of the babymother, because the acting mother is regarded as "growing" the child analogously to the way that the biological mother did in her womb. The acting father who provides food or other support is also regarded as possessing a status like that of the biological father, because both of them are viewed as responsible for "building" the child.[18]

A relatively large number of transitory sexual liaisons, a large proportion of children born out of wedlock, and a family system that, by emphasizing nurturance, rather easily accommodates to changes in membership form a congruent complex of cultural features in Jamaica. There is room for disagreement, but I believe that neither the large number of sexual liaisons nor the obliging nature of the family system provides important explanations for the island's historically high ratio of nonmarital births. More likely, both of these variables are consequences sharing the same precursor: the low rate with which Jamaicans marry. And there is a good bit of evidence to suggest that low marriage rates on the island are more a function of Jamaicans' adverse economic circumstances than any disinclination to marry.

CAUSES OF LOW MARRIAGE RATES

Marriage Values

The research focusing upon the period between 1950 and 1985 generally concluded that most Jamaicans considered conventional marriages to comprise the ideal living arrangement, *regardless* of whether they personally were married. For example, virtually every mother in Blake's sample of lower-class Jamaicans, few of whom were themselves married, explained her daughter-rearing practices as oriented toward enhancing the girl's eventual matrimony. Both mothers and acting fathers said they tried to closely monitor adolescent daughters, justifying their efforts at vigilant supervision by claiming it would lower the risk of her becoming pregnant and thereby raise the girl's chances for marriage.[19]

When asked whether it was better for people in their positions to marry or just to live with someone, about 80 percent of all of Blake's lower-class respondents, both male and female, selected marriage as the arrangement of choice. Most of the remainder were ambivalent. Almost no one, in other words, thought it was better just to live together, even though most were themselves in such "informal" relationships. Women preferred marriage because they believed they would have more financial security with a husband. Men preferred it because they thought a married woman would take better care of her spouse, house, and children. And significant portions of both sexes also preferred marriage because they believed that married people could expect to be treated with more respect in church, stores, and the larger community. Elisa J. Sobo illustrates this last point by describing how one soon-to-be-bride instructed some young girls in the neighborhood that after her wedding they must call her "*Mistress* MacDonald." Another woman in the community, jealous perhaps, described the uppity bride-to-be as acting "like her didi make patty"—as though her feces were food![20]

In the middle class, Lisa Douglass reports, marriage was a more common practice as well as an ideal. Interestingly, the advantages of marriage over just living together seemed much the same across Jamaicans' class lines. Thus, middle-class women said marriage was better because of the respectability and financial security they believed it offered. Douglass also reports that marriage provides "the measure" against which all heterosexual relations are measured. A steady boyfriend or girlfriend, for example, is called a husband or wife in both middle- and lower-class circles.[21]

The most ambivalent view of marriage was expressed by working-class women employed in Kingston's food-processing, shoe-manufacturing, and garment factories. While they all acknowledged that the status and respectability conferred by marriage were attractive, many of the women were dubious that they would benefit from marriage in a material way. Given Jamaicans' patriarchal values, they assumed that any husbands they might have would expect deference and give little in return. The women believed their own jobs would provide the economic support, and they would still do the shopping, cleaning, and other domestic chores. In short, they saw marriage as a potentially bad deal for a working woman in Jamaica—unless she found a husband who could also contribute to household income.[22]

The preceding descriptions of the value most Jamaicans placed upon marriage is extremely pertinent because it implies that out-of-wedlock births, despite their prevalence, were not preferred. Rather, they ocurred so frequently because unwed people engaged in sexual intercourse without contraceptive aids and did not terminate pregnancies with abortion, and neither pregnancy nor actual childbirth effectively acted as a signal to marry. Why not—if people wished that they could marry? The best answer lies in their lack of economic resources.

Economic Constraints to Marriage

The bulk of the Jamaican population was very poor between 1950 and 1985, and remains so today. In Kingston's many shantytowns, large families live in crowded housing that has been created by partitioning small houses into still smaller apartments. Broken windows, leaking roofs, and cracked walls are commonplace. The residents of the building's apartments share toilet facilities, yard space behind the tenement, and a common room for cooking.[23] Kingston is also a dangerous place, with gangs (called "posses") fighting each other for control of neighborhoods. Its very high murder rate is due to the turf and drug wars of posses and a police force that is quick to shoot people.[24]

In small villages outside the city, people are packed into old, one- and two-room thatched huts with dirt floors and no running water. Near some of the island's large sugar cane fields are company barracks offering single rooms that were intended for use by seasonal male workers, but frequently house entire families.[25] There was a steady stream of migrants from country to town who came with stars in their eyes and figured life *had* to be better in Kingston. One woman remembered how she felt when she first got off the train to Kingston in 1960. All she saw were stray dogs, hungry-looking children, and dilapidated shacks. "Lord, I wanted to go right back. . . . But I was proud in those days, an' I thought I could mek something outta' myself in Kingston."[26] (Twenty-five years later, she was a withered prostitute.)

To marry ordinarily requires, for starters, that people establish their own households. However, because jobs are scarce, especially jobs that pay a living wage, a large proportion of the island's adults cannot afford to leave their parents' homes. Rental apartments are expensive, and both land and building materials are prohibitively priced. Further, many young adults own practically nothing, not even a bed or mattress. As many as four adults sleep horizontally across a bed in poor Kingston neighborhoods. So young women look for a man with a job or money so that their relationship can "lead somewhere," and men, with or without jobs, complain that "women always looking something."[27]

The popular culture of Jamaica makes clear the connection between work, money, and marriage. In the poem "Praises," for example, the popular Jamaican poet Louise Bennett pays tribute to the establishment of the American military base in Jamaica. Named Sandy Gully, the base offers local men an opportunity to work, and that makes it possible for island couples to move from sexual relations to marital relations. In the poem, one woman describes her former cohabitating relationship as living "bad," and praises her boyfriend's job at the base because "as him get de fus week pay" the two of them marry.[28]

The clearest empirical evidence of the connections among economic resources, marriage, and out-of-wedlock births is obtained from studies that have compared these variables across different types of Jamaican communities. Especially noteworthy is anthropologist Edith Clarke's ground-breaking study of three rural villages, circa 1950. Economic resources varied greatly among the agricultural communities she studied, and her data showed fluctuations in marriage and out-of-wedlock rates that were consistent with the economic variations.

In each of the communities Clarke examined, there was one major crop from which most residents earned their livelihoods. She gave fictitious names to these real places, each one reflecting the crop that domi- nated. Sugartown was like the plantations on which Jamaicans once toiled as slaves, but in its modern version the seasonal nature of sugar cane gave it a boom-or-bust quality. There were ample jobs and adequate incomes in season, and almost nothing the rest of the year. Mocca was a community in the island's rugged mountains. People here scratched out a meager living, at best. Finally, there was Orange Grove, located on one of Jamaica's fertile plains, where the community prospered from the sale of oranges and collectively-owned livestock enterprises. A summary of a few of her principal findings, along with brief descriptions of the communities, is presented in table 6.2.[29]

Clarke argued that the link between childbearing and marriage was contingent upon both the amount of income in a community and the stability of that income. People had to feel that they could plan their futures, she contended, before they would establish households. Thus,

Table 6.2
Clarke's Three Communities

Community	% Children under age 15 living with:			
	Married Parents	Unmarried Parents	Mothers Only	All Others
SUGARTOWN Jobs/income fluctuate. Moderate in crop season, subsistence in slow time.	21%	27%	39%	13%
MOCCA Extreme, unabated poverty. Agricultural community in very harsh environment.	24%	32%	38%	6%
ORANGE GROVE Income stable and high. Fertile lands, stock, and an egg cooperative.	55%	10%	19%	16%

Source: Data from appendix in Edith Clarke, *My Mother Who Fathered Me* (London: George Allen & Unwin, Ltd., 1966).

even though there may actually have been somewhat more poverty in Mocca than in Sugartown, she claimed that people's compensation was more uniformly distributed throughout the year in Mocca. It was the instability of income in Sugartown that she believed was as detrimental to marriage and household formation as was the more extreme poverty of Mocca.

However, we must note that differences between Mocca and Sugartown in several marriage and out-of-wedlock indicators, including those summarized in table 6.2 were small. And they seem especially small in relation to the large differences between either of these communities and Orange Grove. The latter is the only community in which a majority of children live with married parents and the only one of the three in which single mother–children households are not the most prevalent type.

Similar inferences about the effect of the amount and stability of income can be drawn from studies of different urban neighborhoods in Jamaica. For example, Diane Austin has compared two sections of Kingston: Selton Town and Vermount. The latter was a largely white-collar community, most of whose residents had more than a primary-school education. Their wages tended to be moderate and relatively stable. Most residents of Selton Town, by contrast, were less educated, and they worked in factories or in service jobs. They earned less on average than Vermount residents, and their employment was subject to more fluctuations. As in the rural communities studied by Clarke, the lesser affluence and lower stability of employment in Selton Town was associated with lower marriage rates and higher out-of-wedlock rates than in Vermount.[30]

In sum, we have traced out-of-wedlock rates in Jamaica between roughly 1950 and 1985. More than two in three births were already nonmarital by 1950, yet the proportion increased by about 20 percent over the next thirty-five years. While we recognize that a diminution of marriage may be a lingering legacy of slavery, the *increase* in out-of-wedlock births seems better explained by the continuing inability of the island's economy to provide entry-level jobs for young people, men in particular. This is a vicious cycle: poverty keeps the marital rate low because people lack the resources to establish their own households, but the subsequent high rate of nonmarital births helps to perpetuate poverty.

AFTER 1985: DESPAIR CONTINUES

The absence of job opportunities has disillusioned many of Jamaica's young males, who do not ever expect to find legitimate employment and have quit looking for it. When the domestic sale and transshipment of cocaine and other drugs increased after around 1980, many young men on the island regarded it as providing their best economic opportunity, despite the risks. As one young prisoner explained to Bernard Headley, life in the street outside the walls offered nothing. "Mi 'ready dead," so, he asked rhetorically, "What more dem can do me?"[31]

Perhaps this young prisoner had nothing more to lose, but the consequences of the violence have been terrible for most people on the island, especially in Kingston, as posses have fought over drug-distribution territories. Residents of the city's neighborhoods fell asleep to the sound of shooting, and for them to get to many public facilities, such as Kingston's Public Hospital, they had to dash through streets peppered with nightly barrages of gunfire.[32] Prisons, police, and other criminal-justice-system expenses have correspondingly increased, diverting a larger share of Jamaica's economy into these nonproductive uses. And as the quality of life has deteriorated because of the crime and violence, young people increasingly find Kingston's shantytowns not conducive to planning futures together.

To complete our argument, we now turn to an examination of the general relationship between violence and economic opportunity. In Jamaica, as in many other contemporary nations with high crime rates, the high rates have many potential causes: crowded cities, poverty, number of males aged 15–29 (the peak ages for criminal activity), et cetera. Steven Messner analyzed a sample of fifty-two nations for which he was able to obtain homicide rates from INTERPOL and other data from the United Nations and other sources. This was a highly diverse sample of nations throughout the world.

The analysis showed that almost all the potential causes identified above had some effect on nations' homicide rates, but the single best predictor of any nation's rate was its level of economic discrimination. The greater the relative number of people who are categorically excluded from their country's mainstream economy because of their skin color, language, or other group characteristic, the greater the amount of internal violence. The deprivations and disadvantages experienced by members of the dispossessed group lead to pent-up aggression, Messner explains. The diffuse hostility this produces is expressed in criminal violence that is directed against any targets that happen to be convenient. Jamaica provides an interesting, but in no way unusual, case with both extensive economic restriction and a homicide rate that is among the very highest in the world.[33]

In conclusion, the relative exclusion of the dark-skinned majority from Jamaica's economy has had multiple adverse consequences for the nation, including very high rates of poverty, homicide, and nonmarital births. It is hard to imagine how any legislative action or policy enactment could meaningfully reduce the island's out-of-wedlock birthrate without directly addressing the underlying cause of Jamaica's diverse social problems, namely, the economic exclusion of the black majority.

NOTES

1. For further discussion of Jamaica's colonial history, see Mary M. Carley, *Jamaica* (New York: Praeger, 1963) and Arthur L. Stinchcombe, *Sugar Island Slavery in the Age of Enlightenment* (Princeton, NJ: Princeton University Press, 1995).

2. See the discussion in chapter 2 in Bernard Headley, *The Jamaican Crime Scene* (Washington, DC: Howard University Press, 1996).

3. For a brief period in the 1970s there was a "black is beautiful" movement that temporarily altered these standards, but by the 1980s the traditional preferences had reappeared. See Laurie Gunst, *Born Fi' Dead* (New York: Henry Holt, 1995), p. 28.

4. For further discussion of that movement, see M. G. Smith, *West Indian Family Structure* (Seattle: University of Washington Press, 1962).

5. Orlando Patterson, *Slavery and Social Death* (Cambridge, MA: Harvard University Press, 1982).

6. European traders and missionaries observed that many of the African villages from which they took their slaves were polygamous. They interpreted the presence of (some) African men's multiple wives out of context, and in accordance with their own European cultural views, concluded that African women were inferior, even in their own societies. This interpretation made it easier to condone the slave women's harsh treatment at the hands of white masters. Barbara Bush, *Slave Women in Caribbean Society* (Bloomington, IN: Indiana University Press, 1990).

7. The amount of freedom given to Caribbean slaves—to marry and raise children, for example—also varied. It was lowest for those who worked on sugar plantations, whose owners were well organized; but the point is, lack of control over their own lives was not a uniform experience for Jamaican slaves. See Arthur L. Stinchcombe, "Freedom and Oppression of Slaves in the Eighteenth-Century Caribbean," *American Sociological Review*, 59, Dec. 1994.

8. Carolyn Cooper, *Noises in the Blood* (Durham, NC: Duke University Press, 1995), p.32.

9. A similar argument, not considered here, places more emphasis upon the African cultural traditions of the Jamaicans. In my opinion, the criticisms of legacy-of-slavery explanations apply to such arguments as well. However, it is also true that viewing out-of-wedlock births in Jamaica from an Afrocentric perspective would alter our view of such births and suggest different ways of viewing gender and class on the island. For further discussion, see Niara Sudarkasa, " 'The Status of Women' in Indigenous African Societies," *Feminist Studies*, 12, Spring 1986, and Sharon Elise, "Teenaged Mothers," in Bette J. Dickerson (Ed.), *African American Single Mothers* (Thousand Oaks, CA: Sage Publications, 1995).

10. Elisa J. Sobo, *One Blood* (Albany, NY: State University of New York Press, 1993), p. 179.

11. For further discussion of upper-class courtship and marriage in Jamaica, see Lisa Douglass, *The Power of Sentiment* (Boulder, CO: Westview Press, 1992).

12. Cooper, chapter six.

13. Judith Blake, *Family Structure in Jamaica* (New York: Free Press 1961), chapter six.

14. A. Lynn Bolles, *Sister Jamaica* (Lanham, MD: University Press of America, 1996), chapter six.

15. Blake, p. 91.

16. Ibid., p. 217.

17. For further discussion, see Edith Clarke, *My Mother Who Fathered Me* (London: George Allen & Unwin Ltd., 1966), and Bolles.

18. For further discussion, see Anna S. Meigs, "Blood Kin and Food Kin," in James P. Spradley and David W. McCurdy, *Conformity and Conflict* (Glenview, IL: Scott, Foresman, 1990), and Sobo.

19. Blake, chapter five.

20. Sobo, p. 196.

21. Among the Jamaican elite, however, marriage is tied to the reproduction of status, that is, perpetuating one's lineage. See Douglass.

22. Bolles.

23. Diane J. Austin, *Urban Life in Kingston, Jamaica* (New York: Gordon and Breach, 1984).

24. See Gunst, Part One, and Headley.

25. Clarke, p. 23.

26. Gunst, p. 25.

27. Sobo, p. 194. Around 1980, a leading Jamaican singer named Super-Cat had a big hit called "Boops." It told how women needed a sugar daddy, and "Boopism" became code for the dependency of poor Jamaican women. See Gunst.

28. Quoted in Cooper, p. 55.

29. The communities she studied were real places, but she gave them fictitious names that represent their predominant livelihoods. The children in the "all others" category lived with a variety of others, including fathers, siblings, nonkin, and so forth.

30. See Austin.

31. Headley, p. 21.

32. Gunst, Part One.

33. Steven F. Messner, "Economic Discrimination and Societal Homicide Rates," *American Sociological Review*, 54, Aug. 1989.

PART 3

SOME CONCLUSIONS ABOUT
THE UNITED STATES

In this final section we again turn our attention to the United States, but from a broader perspective than we could muster when we described out-of-wedlock patterns in the United States in part 1. Chapter 7 presents an overview of theoretical approaches. It elaborates upon several major perspectives, including: epidemic theory, traditional family values, rational choice, and Wilson's theory of work and marriage. We are now able to examine the congruence between each of these theoretical views and the out-of-wedlock patterns in the United States as well as in Essex-Terling, Madrid, and Jamaica. In chapter 7 we will also examine the absence of any appreciable increase in Japan's out-of-wedlock rates and consider Japan's uniqueness in this regard in relation to assumptions from several of the theoretical perspectives.

The role of welfare as an inducement to unwed women is the one major theoretical perspective that is not discussed in chapter 7 because it is reasonably clear that welfare or equivalent programs were not an important antecedent to the increases in out-of-wedlock births that occurred in any of the earlier places discussed in part 2. In addition, contemporary welfare reform in the United States is explicitly dedicated to reducing nonmarital births, and how this target should be reached has been the object of major policy debates. Therefore, in order to focus upon the diverse aspects of the relationship between welfare and out-of-wedlock births in the United States we examine welfare in a separate, final chapter.

7

A Theoretical Overview

It is time to try to view the past chapters' descriptions of out-of-wedlock birth patterns in the United States and other societies in relation to some more encompassing theoretical perspectives. We will not confine ourselves to the previously reviewed societies, though they do provide the information that we will emphasize in this theoretical synthesis. In the following pages, we will consider several major theories that offer some insight in our efforts to explain increases in out-of-wedlock births, but each of the theories also seems somewhat limited when it is assessed in light of the several case studies.

EPIDEMIC THEORY

The increase in out-of-wedlock births in the United States in the late twentieth century seemed so precipitous that some observers of the trend described it as acting like an epidemic, and attempted to explain it (as well as other social problems) with a theory of epidemics. We reviewed out-of-wedlock figures for the United States in earlier chapters, so at this point a brief reminder will do. In the mid-1940s about 10 of every 1,000 unmarried women had a child in any year, and that rate increased to about 45 per 1,000 in the mid-1990s. Similarly, looking only at infants, about 1 in 20 was born out of wedlock yearly in the mid-1940s, compared to about 1 in 3 in the mid-1990s. Even in the face of all kinds of marital and family changes that were occurring simultaneously, the increase in nonmarital births still stood out. For example, in

1970, a single parent living with a child under age 18 was five times more likely to be divorced than never married. By 1994, however, single parents were equally likely to be divorced or never married.[1]

According to the theoretical perspective designed to explain epidemics of social phenomena, small changes in some points along a continuum are associated with very large effects, while at other points on the same continuum a large change will have very small effects. In everyday life we experience this sort of thing when we smack the bottom of an upside-down ketchup bottle. One hit, and nothing happens; a second hit with the same force, and a little watery ketchup dribbles out. One more hit, just a little bit harder, and whoosh—out comes more ketchup than we wanted. Malcolm Gladwell recounts the following verse to sum up the way this works:

> Tomato ketchup in a bottle—
> None will come and then the lot'll.[2]

In other words, a very small increase in the force with which the bottle was hit on the third try led to a very large increase in the amount of ketchup that came out.

Epidemic theory is the latest version of a group of "contagion" theories that have examined the way many phenomena creep along incrementally until they reach a critical juncture, after which their increases surge at an accelerated rate. For example, the number of individual patents that were issued leading to many major inventions, including telephones, automobiles, and airplanes, all grew gradually over time until they reached a threshold point, and then the number virtually exploded.[3] In other words, as the wealth of knowledge about the phenomenon accumulated, inventors were able to combine the known facts in an exponentionally growing number of new ways.

Jonathan Crane illustrates how social epidemics are currently viewed by examining changes in neighborhoods. Specifically, he is interested in quantifying the "Neighborhood Quality," or NQ, of relatively poor communities in large cities. The defining measure is the number of high-status workers—accountants, executives, store owners, and so forth—that live in these generally low-status neighborhoods. The lower the percentage of high-status persons living in the neighborhood, the lower its NQ. Neighborhoods with very low NQ scores are true ghettos, he contends. The absence of some high-status persons who could serve as offsetting models or provide assistance makes the uniformly disadvantaged residents of ghettos susceptible to experiencing a wide variety of social problems.

Of most relevance to us is Crane's analysis of teenage childbearing, at least three-quarters of which is out of wedlock. He prepared a graph on which he plotted the NQ and the teen childbearing probabilities in a sample of big-city neighborhoods. He found that as NQ fell, there were increases in teen childbearing, but the increments were very small until NQ reached a tipping point. (The tipping points were somewhat different for black and for white teenagers.) Then further declines of a small magnitude in NQ led to eruptions in nonmarital birth rates. For example, as long as NQ was at least 7.5 (i.e., the neighborhood was comprised of at least 7.5 percent high-status persons) the teen childbearing probability of white teenagers in the neighborhood remained less than 1 in 100. Declines in NQ from more than 30 down to 7.5 obviously had very little effect on teen births. A decline in NQ only from 7.5 to 3.5, however, was associated with a large jump in the probability of teen childbearing among white females in the neighborhood, specifically from 1 in 100 to 1 in 10.[4]

Applications of epidemic theory have examined rates of various behavior in neighborhoods: school dropouts, urinating on subways, vandalism—and teenage childbirth. One reason for the neighborhood focus is that people presumably know what is going on in their neighborhoods, and for contagion to occur, people must be aware of others' actions. A second reason is that many rates of people's behavior are tabulated by neighborhood, so it is possible for an investigator to examine variations within large samples of neighborhoods and thereby identify tipping points.

One could, in principle, look at places larger than neighborhoods and ask whether fluctuations in their out-of-wedlock birthrates (and/or ratios) were consistent with contagion or epidemic theory models. To examine epidemic theory at this level, in addition to out-of-wedlock rates, one would need to identify an independent variable analogous to NQ. It could pertain to rates of employment, the number of times certain themes were presented on television shows, educational levels, or the like. However, no such variable is readily available for the counties, cities, and nations we described in prior chapters. In its absence, one could still examine nonmarital birth patterns over time for consistency with a contagion theory, though. To be specific, extremely large and very steep increases in the nonmarital birth rate would be expected to occur at certain points along the continuum, after a tipping point was reached.

The rapid acceleration of the out-of-wedlock rate in the United States between about 1960 and 1990 was consistent with a contagion model. Steep rate increases in the county of Essex in England circa 1600 and in Madrid, Spain, circa 1800 were also compatible with this model. Furthermore, contagion is typically assumed to operate by peer pressure. That is, theorists expect that people will be most likely to model their behavior according to the standards they see emerging among their peers. In our discussion of Madrid's young people, in particular, we noted that out-of-wedlock rates increased in conjunction with peer pressures encouraging sexual boldness. The county of Essex presented a complex case with respect to peer pressure. The young people who frequented the alehouses and were apparently guilty of numerous sexual and nonsexual offenses may have responded to each other's deviance, and this could have increased out-of-wedlock birthrates. On the other hand, the overall historical pattern of steady but unspectacular increases in out-of-wedlock births in Jamaica totally lacks the sharp inclines and declines that one would expect to be associated with a contagion model.

We can, in sum, offer partial support for a contagion or epidemic theory.[5] It certainly would be interesting to see whether a tipping point could be found for out-of-wedlock births in social units larger than neighborhoods. What makes epidemic theory especially worth exploring further is the possibility that it could offer strategic applications for reducing the incidence of out-of-wedlock births. At the practical core of epidemic theory is the notion that all interventions are not equal in their potential impact. For example, trying to reduce an independent variable that is sustaining a level of out-of-wedlock births well above the tipping point would probably not be effective strategy in terms of return on cost or effort. The interventions with the most leverage would be in neighborhoods or societies that were near their tipping points. Programs would then only have to induce small changes in order to have large effects.

Reasonable people differ, however, in terms of where they think interventions should occur and the form that they should take. For some analysts, it is a weakening of traditional family values that has made the at-risk population susceptible to an epidemic of out-of-wedlock births. Their corresponding strategy is to strengthen traditional families so they can impart traditional family values. For other observers, the traditional family has become an anachronism, and it is time for the state to intervene innovatively. The theoretical underpinnings of these two arguments clash, making their juxtaposition especially interesting. We will examine each in turn.

TRADITIONAL FAMILY VALUES

Advocates of traditional family values contend that it is a mistake to view the increase in out-of-wedlock births as an isolated phenomenon, because it is part of a set of interrelated trends including: more tolerance of premarital and extramarital sexual activity; increased separation and divorce, even when young children are involved; and more reliance upon nonfamilial agents, such as day-care centers and school social workers, in the raising of children. In the contemporary United States, proponents argue, only intact and functioning families can impart traditional family values to children. When these values are not transmitted to succeeding generations, out-of-wedlock births (and extramarital relations, divorce, and so forth) can be expected to increase. So a vicious cycle is enacted: single moms fail to teach traditional family values, leading to more single moms who fail to teach traditional values, leading to . . . and so on.

Two of the principal spokespersons for this position are a former vice president, Dan Quayle, and a former secretary of education, William J. Bennett.[6] They argue that institutions outside of the family, including public schools, government programs, and the mass media, all fail to support traditional values. A modern family must, therefore, be like a fortress that protects members, especially children, from hostile cultural forces while carrying out its socialization responsibilities without external help.

Television, because of its omnipresence, has been singled out for special criticism by advocates of traditional family values. They have focused in particular upon the content of early evening programs (shows in "the family hour," between 8 and 9 P.M. Eastern Time). An analysis of these shows on the major networks during the 1996 season, presumably a pretty typical year, found that the sitcoms that dominated the time slot (*Friends, Mad about You, Wings*) typically revolved around sexual themes. To the audience, they conveyed a picture of unmarried people frantically seeking sexual relations in a nonjudgmental social network. A four-week analysis of these 1996 shows by the Center for Media and Public Affairs counted forty episodes in which unmarried partners engaged in sexual relations—and five in which the partners were married.[7]

When children appeared or were discussed on these shows, they were infrequently living with both parents, but their place in the plots varied. Sometimes they acted as lures for attracting persons of the opposite sex for their single parent. Other times they were impediments to their single parent's ability to carry out sexual affairs. For example, during the same season a main character on *Bless This House* discussed a friend who wanted to get her children out of the house for a while, "so she can do it on the coffee table."[8]

On the one hand family-hour television shows, movies, sex-education courses, government leaders, and public-school teachers apparently placed less emphasis upon traditional family values. On the other hand, adolescents were simultaneously engaging in sexual relations at younger ages, and out-of-wedlock birthrates, especially among the young, were increasing. But did more liberal standards in some meaningful way cause these changes in young people's behavior? Or were the more permissive values and the increased sexual behavior connected in some other way? It is very difficult to reach a conclusion regarding the United States because so many things in addition to traditional values were changing at about the same time. Fortunately, from the previous case studies, there are other places and times we can assess.

In Madrid in the late eighteenth century (see chapter 5) we did see some evidence of a correlation between changing cultural values and the rate with which infants were born out of wedlock as indicated by admissions to the Inclusa. Popular plays and novels imported from France and Italy were presenting Madrid's upper class with more liberal ideas about relations between men and women and nonmarital sexual activity as the rate of nonmarital births increased. At the same time, the boldness and sexual openness of the *majo* and *maja* presented new cultural ideals in the lower class. However, in both the county of Essex circa 1600 (see chapter 4) and in Jamaica more recently (see chapter 6) there was little to suggest that any change in people's values might have corresponded with the increase in out-of-wedlock rates. To the contrary, traditional marriage seems to have remained the exemplar for which people strove, but for economic reasons they were unable to attain it. We did see some evidence, however, that more vigorous religious and civic proscriptions against nonmarital births may have been one of the variables that contributed to a subsequent downturn in Essex's out-of-wedlock rates.

In sum, the evidence pertaining to the role of traditional values is mixed. It does appear that liberalization of people's values is not a necessary precondition to increased rates of nonmarital childbearing. Our case studies indicate that these rates can vary without corresponding fluctuations in values when people's circumstances change. And why would that surprise anyone? Values—in the abstract—are probably not a good predictor of how people will behave, especially if people confront unexpected life situations.

Arland Thornton's research on divorce illustrates this point about values and behavior. He examined six waves of women included in the longitudinal Detroit Area Study. At the onset he measured how the women felt about divorce: Was it wrong? What if children were involved? Over the next eighteen years of the study, some of the women married, and some divorced. Thornton went back to the original interviews to see if there was any correlation between their initial attitudes toward divorce and what they subsequently did. There was not; women who approved and disapproved of divorce were equally likely to have been divorced over the eighteen-year period. Whether or not they divorced depended upon the circumstances they confronted, not their preexisting values. When women with initially disapproving attitudes experienced unsurmountable difficulties in their marriage, Thornton concluded, they either made divorce fit within their existing values or adjusted their attitudes.[9]

The more interesting (and problematic) question for us to consider may be how far traditional values can go in regulating out-of-wedlock births, if those values are institutionalized. To address this question, modern Japan represents an extremely pertinent case study, because law and custom in every institutional sphere tend to reflect traditional family values.

Japan's Experience

In the late 1940s, immediately after World War II, Japan's nonmarital birth ratio surged to about 10 percent. No earlier figures are available for the nation, but this almost certainly represented a very large increase. It was due, on the one hand, to nonmarital births fathered by soldiers in occupying armies and, on the other hand, to very low rates of marriage and marital births among the war-ravaged Japanese. By 1960, however, the nation's out-of-wedlock ratio was down to 1 percent, which was probably similar to its prewar ratio, and it has remained virtually unchanged since then, at least through the mid-1990s.[10]

Table 7.1
Out-of-Wedlock Ratios, 1960 to 1992

1-2% Ratios in 1960	1992 Ratios (%)
JAPAN	1
Italy	7
Spain	10
Netherlands	12
4–6% Ratios in 1960	
Australia	24
Canada	29
United States	30
United Kingdom	31
France	33

Note: "Ratios" refers to nonmarital births as a percentage of all births.

Source: Data from Daniel Patrick Moynihan, "The Great Transformation," American Enterprise, 6 (1995), figure 3.

To put Japan into comparative perspective, table 7.1 examines two groups of nations' out-of-wedlock ratios, circa 1960 and 1992. In the first category are nations that scored very low in 1960. Japan was among them. In the second category are nations that scored moderately, including the United States. (Not shown in the table is a small and diverse group of high-scoring Scandinavian nations.[11])

Table 7.1 makes clear that, to a large extent, 1992 ratios were a function of 1960 scores. Every nation tended to remain in the same relative category, despite scoring higher in 1992 than in 1960. A dramatic exception to the increase in 1992 scores was Japan, whose ratios did not increase at all.

There are a number of variables that contribute to Japan's low rate, but the most important is probably the way unwed mothers are shamed by both family and peers and openly discriminated against in school, work, apartment rentals, and government taxes. In almost all of these regards, Japan stands in marked contrast to the United States, but not because Japan is generally more puritanical in its attitudes. To judge from national surveys, the percentage of adults who disapprove of premarital and extramarital relations is nearly identical in both countries. Marked differences occur where children are involved, though. For example, significantly fewer Japanese (36 percent) than Americans (57 percent) agree that "one parent can bring up a child as well as two parents together." Correspondingly, more Japanese than Americans say they believe that parents should stay married even if they are not happy together.[12]

The strong preference for two-parent families translates into numerous condemnations if a single woman becomes visibly pregnant in Japan. Parents and other relatives will typically withhold any help, and they may even shun her. If she is a high-school student, she will likely be expelled. There are strong pressures on unmarried women to quietly seek abortions. Appreciating these circumstances, many Japanese physicians perform abortions without parental notification, even though technically they should not. One pregnant 19-year-old woman said she nearly fainted when her doctor said he would need a letter from her parents. He ultimately relented when she explained, "If my parents even knew that I have a boyfriend, they wouldn't let me go out of the house."[13]

If an unmarried woman nevertheless decides to have the baby and keep it, then her problems, and her child's, really begin. Landlords will discriminate against her, and she will find it difficult to find a decent place for herself and her child to live. Many companies will refuse to hire her if they know she is a single mother. Then there is Japan's tax policy, which is intended to penalize women who choose to become parents outside of marriage. Women with children who later divorce or become widowed receive substantial tax deductions against their income, deductions worth several thousand dollars on average. Never-married mothers do not receive this deduction, which means they pay higher national and local income taxes—plus higher fees for public day care and health insurance, because those taxes and fees are based upon people's adjusted gross income.[14]

For children born out of wedlock, their parent's status is a permanent part of their official government records and their identity in the community. Years later they may be denied admission to prominent schools because they are fatherless, and their attractiveness as a marriage partner is diminished. When they die, relatives may refuse to enshrine their ashes.

In sum, from cradle to grave, across every institution, Japanese values condemning unwed motherhood are backed up with severe condemnations for those who deviate and for their offspring. The humiliation and punishment that women can anticipate seem to have been quite effective in helping to keep Japan's out-of-wedlock rate way below that of other contemporary nations.

In the United States, tax and welfare policies as well as school and work practices are all markedly different from Japan's in their treatment of unwed mothers. Parents who are divorced and widowed or were never married all tend to be treated alike in the United States, if their other social attributes are the same. The failure to discriminate against women who, up front, chose single motherhood has, in the opinion of some analysts, encouraged women to become single mothers, or at least has failed to discourage them. We will later examine the facts and arguments surrounding U.S. policies in some detail. First, however, we turn to a very different theoretical conception of modern societies in which neither traditional families nor traditional values are expected to occupy a very important place.

RATIONAL CHOICE

Throughout most of the eighteenth century, Western societies were primarily comprised of independent households. Most of the people worked on small farms and were governed largely by tradition. The family was the primary social unit, in that all important activities were either part of families or erected over the structures of families. Then, of course, there were revolutionary changes in the world: cities grew and became the dominant centers of social and economic life, non-family-based production grew and evolved into large-scale industry, and the mass media joined mass production.

Of particular significance, according to James Coleman, was the social invention of a "corporate actor." Private firms and corporations, schools, units of government, and voluntary organizations all became recognized as noncorporal actors that had legal rights and responsibilities. For example, town governments can be sued for negligence, and private companies can be sued for discrimination; if found guilty, either can be fined. Coleman refers to the earlier type of social organization, in which families were the central unit and tradition predominated, as "primordial." The contemporary form, which uniquely possesses the concept of corporate actors, he calls purposively constructed social organization.[15]

In addition to the differences already noted, Coleman emphasizes the distinguishing types of social control each type of social organization employs. In purposively constructed organizations, the corporate actor makes formal rules, sets impersonal sanctions for violations, and offers performance incentives. In a primordial social organization, by contrast, the primary modes of social control are (1) norms that rest upon informal consensus, (2) people's concern with their reputation in the group, and (3) ongoing reciprocity.[16]

Each type of social control operates well within the type of social organization that it fits. Problems arise, Coleman continues, when primordial modes are employed in purposively constructed organizations. They usually do not work well because people do not tend to remain permanently in purposively constructed organizations and because people's roles in such organizations ordinarily encompass only small parts of their lives. To illustrate, consider how the three principal modes of primordial control might fail to operate in a purposively constructed organization, like a modern workplace.

1. Norms based upon informal consensus cannot be counted upon because co-workers may very well not share the same views, or may not work together long enough for consensus to develop.
2. Reputations in the work group may be insignificant to participants compared to their standing in their profession, local community, or church.
3. The possibility that one's actions will invite reciprocity may not be much of a consideration if people do not plan to stay long enough to give others an opportunity to square accounts.

The critical mistake we have been making as a society, in Coleman's view, is not realizing the full implications of living in a purposively constructed world. What is called for is "the explicit design of institutions, rather than the mere patching up of old ones."[17] And one of Coleman's leading candidates for reconstruction is the family, or the institution charged with raising children. Given the way primordial social organization has been replaced all around us, it is hardly surprising that the traditional family has "rapidly disintegrated" and that most of its primary child-rearing functions have been delegated outside of the household.

With respect to institutional design, Coleman's rational-choice approach entails explicit evaluation of the benefits and costs associated with institutional forms. The assumption is that over the long run and in the aggregate, people's behavior will be consistent with self-interests. Gary Becker's analysis of fertility rates provides an interesting example. Children on farms, he begins, have historically performed more chores and contributed more to family income than children in cities. In rural areas this increased the demand for children, like any other commodity, which provides the reason that farm families were larger in size than city families for several hundred years. When agriculture became more mechanized, youngsters needed more schooling in order to be productive, but rural schools were too small to be efficient. Regional schools were the answer, but they involved greater expenditures, including costs for time and transportation. The expenses associated with schooling lowered the demand for children on farms, and that is why, Becker concludes, rural-urban fertility differences disappeared.[18] In addition, Coleman writes, neither rural nor urban parents any longer count on children to support them in old age, and this has lowered the value of children to parents everywhere. The problem, Coleman concludes, is that no one has much incentive to raise children who can later be of maximum value to society. American parents no longer do, and day-care centers and the public schools never did. The one (corporate) actor that now has a strong interest in maximizing the value of a child to the society is the state. The more productive children become, the more they contribute to the state in taxes and the less they cost the state, in terms of expenditures related to crime and incarceration, welfare, and so forth. As the traditional family disintegrates, it cannot be counted on to prevent children from running wild or going off and doing their own thing. Carrying on family honor is not meaningful anymore. Self-interest is, so Coleman's solution is to develop formulas by which the state can give a claim against a child's future earnings to parents or foster parents, schools, and perhaps other specially designed corporate actors.[19]

In some respects, the traditional-family-values approach stands in such sharp juxtaposition to rational-choice assumptions that it is hard to imagine how they could ever be combined. Following Coleman, one would probably argue against efforts to revitalize the traditional family because that would be seen as trying to patch up a (primordial) form that no longer fits in our purposively constructed society. Only the rational design of new institutional forms, according to Coleman, could lead to an optimum solution of society's child-rearing problem. In addition, the two theoretical approaches make very different assumptions about what motivates human behavior. The advocates of the traditional-family-values position place great reliance upon the capacity of internalized standards to guide people. That is why they stress the centrality of the socialization process. Rational-choice theorists, by contrast, prefer to emphasize the importance of the proper structuring of external incentives, believing that people will follow their own self-interest.[20]

On the other hand, it may be possible to see aspects of these two seemingly different approaches operating in combination with each other. In Essex and Madrid, for example, we saw evidence that parents of grown children placed a monetary premium on maintaining family honor. Thus, a daughter and her boyfriend could sometimes put pressure on her father in their dowry negotiations if she was pregnant. In other words, traditional family values motivated people to induce their offspring to have marital rather than nonmarital births.

Reconsider also the case of modern Japan, where traditional family values still seem to be working to limit out-of-wedlock births. Could their continued effectiveness be a result of the fact that Japanese children (sons, in particular) still have obligations to support elderly parents? That could provide Japanese parents with strong incentives to raise children to be productive citizens, and given Japan's institutionalized value system that discriminates against children born out-of-wedlock and their parents, it is simply not in the interest of Japanese women or men to have children outside of marriage. So perhaps a value system is effectively institutionalized when corporate actors offer incentives that motivate people to comply with value standards while they are simultaneously pursuing their self-interest.[21]

WORK AND MARRIAGE

The final theoretical position we will examine in this chapter is associated most closely with the writings of William J. Wilson. Although he is now a professor at Harvard, most of his writings were published while he was at the Sociology Department of the University of Chicago, and his observations and interviews were conducted primarily in Chicago's inner-city black neighborhoods. The theory he presents is most applicable to the residents of large, inner-city black ghettos in the Midwest and Northeast. However, it is not entirely confined to them. Whites living in the inner core of large cities have experienced similar problems; so, too, have blacks living in smaller cities and in other regions of the country.

Let us begin with an examination of Wilson's primary target group. African Americans are only about 11 percent of American society. As such, they rarely constitute a majority of the persons in any statistical category, and that includes out-of-wedlock births. From the data provided on birth certificates in 1993, for example, it appears that blacks accounted for about 36 percent of all nonmarital births.[22] In proportion to the relative sizes of the at-risk populations, the black contribution to out-of-wedlock births was about three times greater than would be expected (if there were no racial differences).

Blacks are overrepresented because within the black population, non-marital childbearing has overwhelmed marital childbearing. As described in chapter 2, over three-quarters of all black women who had their first child in 1994 had never been married, and the percentage of black children living with the mother only—a statistical majority since 1990—continues to rise. How quickly this has changed: in 1970, fewer than 30 percent of black children lived with the mother only.[23]

Given blacks' extremely high rates of out-of-wedlock births, it seems reasonable for theories to focus upon their relevant experience. Further, given the similarities in nonmarital birth patterns among blacks and whites—both have higher rates in large cities and among younger and less well educated women—any theory that explained how rates increased among blacks would likely not be limited only to blacks. We turn now to Wilson's theory.

Wilson's Theory

Between about 1960 and the mid-1980s, an occupational transformation occurred in many of the larger U.S. cities, especially in the Northeast and Midwest. Manufacturing firms, with their relatively high-paying jobs, moved south and west, to smaller towns, or else left the nation entirely. Little of the urban population most immediately affected followed the jobs, though; they remained behind. The resulting disequilibrium or mismatch in the supply of and demand for urban labor left northern inner cities with markedly higher levels of unemployment.[24] This disequilibrium was especially ill timed because large numbers of baby boomers were simultaneously reaching maturity and trying to enter the labor market.

Wilson contended that manufacturing jobs had been the major source of high-paying employment for black males with limited education.[25] Taking their shifts in the steel mills or automobile assembly plants, they could support a family in respectable working-class style. However, the jobs that were generated replacing manufacturing in central cities tended to exclude blacks, and black males in particular, for one of two reasons. First, there were high-status positions in finance and banking, but they required more education than most of the inner-city residents possessed. Second, there were low-paying service jobs, such as putting hamburgers in a bag. Black males had the qualifications for these jobs, but employers discriminated against them in favor of black females or whites.

Meanwhile, inner-city communities and their institutions deteriorated. No one wanted to invest money in neighborhood businesses or apartment buildings when there was so much unemployment. Mortgage loans and insurance became virtually impossible to obtain because banks and lending institutions redlined these neighborhoods. The result was a vicious cycle in which those most able to be mobile, by virtue of their education or work record, left these inner-city neighborhoods, and the areas evolved into true ghettos.

The high rates of joblessness among inner-city males shrank the "male marriageable pool," which Wilson defined as the number of males with jobs per 100,000 females. He saw its constriction as responsible for delayed marriages and for increases in the percentage of women who never married or failed to remarry following a divorce. Although not confined to blacks, the shrinkage in the male marriageable pool was especially pronounced among blacks. If for statistical purposes we assume that all blacks intramarry, then for every three never-married black women in their twenties, during most of the 1980s there was only one male with above-poverty income.[26]

With fewer marriages occurring, Wilson continued, there was an increase in the number of out-of-wedlock births.[27] Female-headed households with young children but no male present became the dominant type of inner-city household, and it has been consistently associated with poverty and other social problems, including welfare dependency and violent crime. As these related problems grew, they drove out the remaining persons of higher status and further discouraged neighborhood investment of every type. Soon only liquor stores and check-cashing outlets remained, school buildings deteriorated, parks were abandoned, and the hallways of public housing projects replaced children's playgrounds.

It is easy to view these neighborhoods from an epidemic perspective. For example, a growing number of young, single mothers feel overwhelmed by child-rearing and household responsibilities, so they leave the outside of their dwellings unattended. The appearance of everyone's front porch and door runs down. As residents look around at these conditions, they feel discouraged from investing time or effort into fixing up their own place. Once past the tipping point, Wilson surmises, an entire neighborhood's housing stock can quickly deteriorate.[28]

The black males who grow up in these ghettos are not oriented toward regular work. They do not expect to find jobs, and a work routine does not become a regulating force in their lives. By default, many seek illegitimate sources of income, such as selling drugs. Then sizable numbers shoot each other or wind up in prison, and in either case the pool of *any* men in the neighborhood available for marriage further declines.

However, marriage is not attractive to these men, even when their girlfriends become pregnant. Why get married, Wilson's respondents asked? It will just end in divorce. In the meanwhile, the men were enjoying the "dating market," where they claimed there were at least one-half dozen women for each man. Many of the women said they would, in principle, like to marry, especially if they became pregnant, but they recognized that their boyfriends would make poor husbands and fathers—they were jobless, without encouraging prospects, and preferred to spend their time on the streets rather than at home.[29]

A great many empirical studies have borrowed insights from Wilson's theory of men, women, and work to help explain their findings. It has been enormously influential and very useful despite the fact that it has received relatively few direct and systematic tests. One impediment to research is uncertainty concerning the most appropriate unit of analysis. Neighborhoods seem too small: people are not that confined in seeking jobs or spouses, though what a neighborhood has to offer is important. On the other hand, metropolitan areas seem too large because most have ecological or symbolic boundaries that people do not ordinarily cross. Therefore, what could be available on the other side does not really matter to them. Translating the concept of the male marriageable pool into a concrete measure presents an additional problem for researchers. It could be operationally defined as the proportion of males (in the neighborhood or metropolitan area) or the proportion of men with jobs, or by the average income of those jobs. One might also try to examine men and women according to the marital implications of their age categories, though except for eliminating young children, that would be extremely difficult. In sum, to test Wilson's theory a researcher must make a number of methodological choices, and the decisions that are made are likely to affect the findings that will be obtained.

An especially relevant study was reported by Mark Fossett and Jill Kiecolt. They examined a sample of only blacks and looked at several different indicators of the male marriage pool within metropolitan areas. A ratio of the number of employed males to the total number of females in the metropolitan area and a measure of the average prestige of the males' jobs were both found to be significantly related to the out-of-wedlock ratio. As the number of employed black males increased or as the standing of their jobs increased, the ratio of nonmarital births declined among black females of all ages.[30]

When studies have relied upon other measures of the male marriageable pool, focused upon neighborhoods or entire states rather than metropolitan areas, or taken different samples of people, there have been fluctuations in their results. However, most of the findings have been supportive of Wilson's major hypothesis.[31] Further, the causal path seems to be essentially the same for blacks and for whites when both are in the underclass. While the magnitudes differed, both suffered economically from the loss of manufacturing jobs, the male marriageable pools of both shrank, and the out-of-wedlock birth ratio increased among both.[32].

The economic dislocation argument that Wilson put forward as an explanation for high nonmarital birth ratios during recent times in the United States also fits, and very well, the other places and times discussed in previous chapters. To be specific, extremely high levels of structural unemployment have been a persistent problem in Jamaica, and that nation's out-of-wedlock rates have remained among the very highest in the world. In addition, the more short-lived but rapid increases in out-of-wedlock rates that occurred both in Essex circa 1600 and in Madrid circa 1800 followed severe economic downturns that produced markedly higher levels of unemployment, especially among young people.

Wilson's theory may also help us to understand some aspects of the relationship between women who become single mothers and the men who father their children. In several of the preceding chapters, we encountered evidence that a significant portion of these men were substantially older than the women, and in some instances a coercive element was either implied or apparent. When there was also a marked difference in their status—for example, he employed her as a maid in his household—then the nature of the intimidation is not difficult to understand.

In the absence of a status difference, however, explanations for the age difference and coercive element are less readily apparent until we consider all of the implications of a shrinking male marriageable pool.[33] Whether it constricts as a result of economic dislocations resulting in high unemployment, high rates of male incarceration, or service in an army, one result is the same: the relative number of eligible (or desirable) men declines. As a consequence, the value of a male, like any other commodity, increases. Women may then be more prepared to be intimate with men who they would otherwise consider too old, too low in status, too unattractive, and so forth. The "price," in human terms, a woman is prepared to pay for a relationship with a man may also rise. Thus, men can get away with actions that women would not tolerate in a different demographic marketplace.[34]

There may also be more psychological explanations for men who do not consider themselves in potentially permanent relationships with women but nevertheless intentionally try to father children. On the one hand, the absence of work may deprive these men of more conventional ways of proving their worth. Virility could still be demonstrated, however, by fathering a number of children. On the other hand, Wilson notes that work provides a "framework" for people's daily lives. The work routine imposes discipline and rational planning. These processes and controls may be weakened when long-term unemployment severs men's feelings of connectedness to the formal economy.[35] This may have contributed to high out-of-wedlock rates on the south side of Chicago in 1980; in Kingston, Jamaica, in 1960; and in Madrid, Spain, in 1790.

NOTES

1. For further discussion, and the sources of these figures, see chapter 3.

2. See Malcolm Gladwell, "The Tipping Point," *New Yorker*, June 3, 1996.

3. These examples and others were included in an early statement of this type of theory presented by Robert L. Hamblin, R. Brooke Jacobsen, and Jerry L. Miller, *A Mathematical Theory of Social Change* (New York: Wiley, 1973).

4. Jonathan Crane, "The Epidemic Theory of Ghettos and Neighborhood Effects on Dropping Out and Teenage Childbearing," *American Journal of Sociology*, 96, March 1991, p. 1240.

5. The most troubling aspect of epidemic theory's imagery, for me, concerns the place of human volition. However, it need not imply that this agency is peripheral, as it would be in many conventional applications of epidemic theory, that is, applications to illness or disease.

6. See: William J. Bennett, *The De-Valuing of America* (New York: Summit Books, 1992), and Dan Quayle and Diane Medved, *The American Family* (New York: HarperCollins, 1996).

7. Paul Farhi, "The Racy Race for Ratings," *Washington Post National Weekly Edition*, June 17–23, 1996.

8. Ibid., p. 34.

9. Arland Thornton, "Changing Attitudes toward Separation and Divorce," *American Journal of Sociology*, 90, Jan. 1985.

10. Ministry of Health and Welfare, *Vital Statistics of Japan, 1994* (Tokyo: Statistics and Information Department, 1996), table 3.

11. Figures for these and other nations are presented in Daniel Patrick Moynihan, "The Great Transformation" *American Enterprise*, 6, 1995, figure 3.

12. Everett C. Ladd and Karlyn H. Bowman, *Public Opinion in America and Japan* (Washington, DC: AEI Press, 1996), table 4–7 and 4–24.

13. *New York Times*, March 13, 1996, p. A11.

14. Ibid. However, in other realms, all unmarried mothers do face discrimination to some degree, but less so than never-married mothers.

15. James S. Coleman, "The Rational Reconstruction of Society," *American Sociological Review*, 58, Feb. 1993.

16. His social control theories are further elaborated in James S. Coleman, *Foundations of Social Theory* (Cambridge, MA: Harvard University Press, 1990). See also Jack P. Gibbs, *Control: Sociology's Central Notion* (Urbana, IL: University of Illinois Press, 1989).

17. Coleman, "The Rational Reconstruction of Society," p. 10.

18. Gary S. Becker, *A Treatise on the Family* (Cambridge, MA: Harvard University Press, 1991).

19. Coleman, "The Rational Reconstruction of Society."

20. Some critics contend that because self-interest is a foundation of rational choice, the theory will lead to the design of institutions that will further erode cooperative values and public spiritedness. However, some assessments of actual design projects contend that these feared effects do not necessarily result. See Douglas D. Heckathorn and Robert S. Broadhead, "Rational Choice, Public Policy and Aids," *Rationality and Society*, 8, 1996.

21. This conclusion involves a view of institutionalization that closely resembles the presentation one-half century ago in Talcott Parsons, *The Social System* (New York: Free Press, 1951).

22. Stephanie J. Ventura, Joyce A. Martin and Selma M. Taffel, *Final Natality Statistics, 1993*, National Center for Health Statistics (Washington, DC: GPO, 1995), appendix table I-2. However, I believe that a good deal more attention has been directed at black out-of-wedlock rates because blacks are overrepresented on AFDC (i.e., welfare rolls). This is a separate issue that we will examine in the following chapter.

23. Claudette E. Bennett, *The Black Population in the United States*, Current Population Reports, P20–480 (Washington, DC: GPO, 1995), table F.

24. For further discussion, see John D. Kasarda, "Urban Change and Minority Opportunities," in Paul E. Peterson (Ed.), *The New Urban Reality* (Washington, DC: Brookings Institute, 1985), and John D. Kasarda, "Urban Industrial Transition and the Underclass." *Annals of the American Academy of Political and Social Science*, 501, Jan. 1989.

25. William J. Wilson, *The Truly Disadvantaged* (Chicago: University of Chicago Press, 1987), and William J. Wilson, "Studying Inner-City Social Dislocations," *American Sociological Review*, 56, Feb. 1991.

26. See Daniel T. Lichter, "Race and the Retreat from Marriage," *American Sociological Review*, 57, Dec. 1992, p. 797.

27. Wilson, *The Truly Disadvantaged*.

28. Ibid.

29. William J. Wilson, *When Work Disappears* (New York: Knopf, 1996).

30. Mark A. Fossett and K. Jill Kiecolt, "Mate Availability and Family Structure among African Americans in U.S. Metropolitan Areas," *Journal of Marriage and Family,* 55, May 1993.

31. For a summary of relevant studies, see Greg J. Duncan, "How Nonmarital Childbearing Is Affected by Neighborhoods, Marital Opportunities and Labor Market Conditions," in U.S. Department of Health and Human Services, *Report to Congress on Out-of-Wedlock Childbearing* (Washington, DC: GPO, 1995).

32. Wilson *The Truly Disadvantaged*. He also noted that while his theory seemed most applicable to nonwhites, he did not intend for it to be entirely restricted to nonwhites.

33. See also the discussion in Fossett and Kiecolt.

34. My argument is based upon supply and demand considerations, not gender. Thus, a shortage of females would similarly be expected to work to their advantage vis-à-vis males.

35. Wilson, *When Work Disappears*.

8

Welfare

In past chapters' descriptions of the contemporary United States, we have briefly noted some possible roles that welfare may have played in either causing or sustaining the increase in out-of-wedlock births. Because the issues involved are complex, emotionally charged, and full of social-policy implications, we have deferred discussion of welfare to this separate chapter. It should be noted here that welfare emerges as a variable in the contemporary United States but not in the other places examined in previous chapters. There were no welfare-like or welfare equivalent inducements that could explain out-of-wedlock surges in Essex, Madrid, or Jamaica. Therefore, even if welfare were found to have played an important part in the out-of-wedlock increase in the United States, one should be reluctant to generalize about this finding.

This chapter begins with a historical review of the types of assistance that have been provided in the United States to unmarried women who have children and need help. Over the past one hundred years, sources of support switched from the private to the public sector, and were offered to single-parent families over longer periods of time. We will describe first the large expansion of public benefits, many of which began in the Great Society programs of the 1960s, and then the twenty-five years of welfare reform efforts that followed. This chapter will also include an assessment of whether federally funded aid for families with dependent children (and related benefits) has been a response to the needs of women and children as its supporters have claimed, or has served to entice women into premature motherhood and unproductive lives, as its critics contend.

Before beginning a review of welfare, however, we should explicitly consider the relationships among poverty, dependency, and nonmarital childbearing. Unmarried women with children tend to have high rates of poverty, both before and after they become mothers. As we saw in earlier chapters, these women are disproportionately drawn from a pool of low-education, low-income women. Their family background during their childhood must be partly responsible for their continued poverty and reliance on welfare after they have children of their own.[1] Thus the effect of nonmarital childbearing itself upon poverty and welfare, although substantial, is probably often exaggerated. It is also important to keep clear the distinction between poverty and welfare utilization. Some below-poverty-line families with children that could qualify for public assistance refuse to pursue it on moral grounds. Others do not apply because they are unaware that they are eligible for benefits. So the rolls of welfare recipients cannot be equated with the number of very poor families. The Great Society programs of the 1960s increased the percentage of all children in poverty who received federal and state aid. From 1970 into the 1990s, however, the percentage of poor children whose families received welfare (i.e., AFDC) increased only from 59 percent to 63 percent.[2]

We must also make a distinction between the percentage of children born out of wedlock whose families receive welfare benefits and the percentage of recipient families that are comprised of children and their unmarried mothers. The second figure is easier to calculate because extensive records are kept describing the characteristics of AFDC recipients. In 1993, at least 5 percent of covered children were born to a never-married parent. (Parents' marital status was not known for another 5 percent of the children, and some of the parents of this group were likely to have been unmarried also.[3])

Working in the other direction—the likelihood that the family of a child born out of wedlock will wind up on welfare—presents more difficulties. Unmarried mothers (or fathers) are not a specifically monitored cohort. The best estimates of their welfare utilization come from longitudinal studies with representative samples, including the National Longitudinal Study of Youth (NLSY), discussed in chapter 2. The samples included in most of the longitudinal studies other than NLSY tend not to adequately reflect the welfare subpopulation, and because they were not primarily intended to track welfare, they do not devote a sufficient number of questions to measuring the extent of utilization. Nevertheless, the longitudinal studies provide the best estimates.

The 3,325 women who were in the first and last waves of the NLSY and who bore a child provided the core sample for an interesting analysis reported by Sandra Danziger and Kelleen Kaye. Looking first in terms of children between the ages of 1 and 3 who were born outside of marriage, they report that just under one-half of the children were covered by AFDC between 1988 and 1994. Between 1980 and 1988, the yearly figures hovered between 55 percent and 57 percent. Looking next at the women, among those who were married prior to their first birth, only 5 percent went on AFDC within one year. Among all those women who had never married at first birth, approximately 40 percent went on AFDC within one year.[4] Other studies uniformly suggest that the welfare rates of single mothers continue to cumulate over time, surpassing 50 percent. The rates are especially high for teenagers having nonmarital births. Within five years of an out-of-wedlock birth, over three-quarters of teen mothers are consistently reported to receive AFDC.[5]

In sum, a majority of women who have out-of-wedlock births are likely to be dependent upon welfare at some time, and a majority of welfare (AFDC) recipients are families comprised of children and an unmarried parent. However, the majorities are slim ones, leaving very substantial numbers of women whose lifestyles do not include conventional marriage but nevertheless have children and raise them independently. It is important to remember that we are not talking about these women here.

FROM MATERNITY HOMES TO TANF

At the turn of the twentieth century, when an unmarried woman without means had a child and her family (and the baby's father) would not or could not help, she would turn to private charities. This typically entailed maternity homes run by religious organizations and private philanthropists. These homes took in unwed women in the later stages of pregnancy or the unwed mother and her newborn. The women and their infants were typically residents for as little as a few months to as much as two years. The immediate objective of most homes was to provide shelter, both psychological and physical, for women whose behavior was publicly condemned as shameful. The staff taught the mostly young mothers how to care for themselves and their babies and then tried to integrate mother and child into an external community. Outreach workers contacted her relatives, former neighbors, church members, co-workers, and others, trying to involve as many of them as possible in a rehabilitative plan for the woman. The long-term objective was to ensure that when the resident resumed her noninstitutional life outside of the home, she would not have any more children out of wedlock.[6]

The first non-private benefits for women and children were "mother's pensions." These programs were instituted by most states between 1910 and 1920, and were predicated on the assumption that for women to properly raise children, they had to be free of pressures to work outside the home. Although they defined women's proper roles in a very traditional (at-home) way, "old-girls' networks" of well-connected, high-status women played prominent parts in the development of these plans.[7] From state to state, and among counties within states, there were marked variations in exactly who was covered and how much they were given. However, the benefits were uniformly pretty meager, and 80 percent of all the recipients were widowed white women with children.

The first program of the federal government to provide assistance directly to unmarried mothers was ADC, Aid to Dependent Children, or Title IV of the omnibus Social Security Act of 1935. This act was one important part of the New Deal's response to the Great Depression of the 1930s. Suffering was widespread, of course, and there was special public concern with the plight of women and young children who were in difficult circumstances. Everyone agreed, in 1935, that ADC ought to include children and their mothers who were either widowed, deserted, or married to a man who was unable to work. Their suffering was not considered of their own making. In addition, the act eventually made unmarried women with children eligible for benefits, but that was not the intent of everyone involved in the passage of ADC. One unit within the Department of Labor, the Children's Bureau, advocated for broad coverage and found allies in the Congress. However, the Secretary of Labor, Frances Perkins, later said she had been duped by the Children's Bureau, and that it never occurred to her that out-of-wedlock births would be covered by ADC.[8]

Over the first decade of the program, the percentage of recipient children living with a widowed mother declined from about 80 percent to 20 percent, and nearly one-third of the children who were covered resided with both parents but the father was incapacitated. Only a small number of unmarried women with children received ADC coverage, and many of them were southern blacks. The southern states, left on their own, would have denied them benefits because of their race and their nonmarried status, but the federal government insisted upon their inclusion. The federal reimbursement of states for program costs, which increased during this period, made federal guidelines more difficult for states to ignore.[9]

Through the 1950s, governmental expenditures on ADC increased modestly, and the characteristics of recipients continued to change. By 1961, only 8 percent of the covered children lived with a widowed mother, two-thirds lived in a home where no father was present, and barely over one-half of ADC rolls involved white (non-Hispanic) families. Despite some publicized cases of abuse and fraud, ADC benefits offered to unmarried mothers increased dramatically during the 1960s as part of the "war on poverty" waged in President Lyndon Johnson's Great Society. Further, ADC was supplemented by new Social Security provisions, specifically the Food Stamp program, and Medicaid. Cumulatively, these programs led to a historic reduction in poverty in America.

ADC and its successor, AFDC, were the most visible programs providing payments to dependent families, but most recipients also received benefits from other federal and state programs begun as parts of the Great Society. The size of each of these benefits varied substantially by state and family composition. In 1993, a family with one dependent child in Louisiana or Mississippi, for example, received an AFDC payment of less than $120 per month. In Vermont or Connecticut, by contrast, the same family received about $500 per month. If a child in the family was physically or mentally disabled, though, Supplementary Security Income (SSI) provided payments for that child that were several times larger than AFDC, and unlike AFDC, the size of SSI payments to additional children did not decline in size. There were also Medicaid benefits, which in 1993 covered an average of about $2,500 in medical expenses in AFDC households.[10]

Nearly 90 percent of AFDC recipients also received food stamps in 1993, up to a maximum of about $100 per month; and in some states, Supplementary Food Programs for Women, Infants and Children (WIC) provided milk, cheese, and baby formula worth almost as much as food stamps. Nearly one-quarter of AFDC recipients lived in federally funded (HUD) or state-subsidized housing units, and some states also helped eligible residents pay utility or heating bills.

The number of recipients of ADC and then AFDC benefits increased dramatically during the 1960s, from 3 million at the start of the decade to nearly 9 million by the end of the decade. The steep rate of increase continued into the early 1970s, when the number of recipients reached 11 million. The number stabilized then, fluctuating slightly around 11 million until 1990. Fueled by a recession in 1990, the number of recipients again increased rapidly, topping off at a peak of 14.4 million in 1994. Viewed in terms of recipient families, this represented an increase from about 3.9 million to about 5 million. After reaching this pinnacle, economic growth and job creation helped to produce the sharpest two-year decline in AFDC history as the number of recipients fell back below 12 million by the end of 1996. The number of families on AFDC similarly declined, to about 4.2 million.[11] (The Welfare Reform Act, signed in 1997, officially ended AFDC and replaced it and several other programs with a block grant to states given the acronym TANF (Temporary Assistance to Needy Families).

Measured in constant dollars, the average AFDC benefit paid to families consistently declined between 1970 and the mid-1990s. The drop was especially precipitous—from $665 to $472 per month—between 1970 and 1980, when the number of recipients rose most. Between the mid-1980s and the mid-1990s, the value of AFDC benefits, in constant dollars, continued to slide down, but very gradually. Average payments declined because benefits failed to keep pace with inflation, but also because the average size of a covered family fell from four in the early 1970s to three in the early 1990s. It is difficult to calculate the cash value of non-AFDC benefits at a national level because of local variations in the average cost of rent, food, and so forth. However, if benefits besides AFDC, such as food stamps, are estimated and family size is held constant, the trend looks a little different. Then the value of benefits from year to year, after 1985, seems more unchanging than diminishing.[12]

The changes in the characteristics of dependent families that began with the inception of ADC continued to the demise of AFDC. By the mid-1990s, widowed parents comprised only 1 percent of AFDC households, and well over one-half were not married parents. In addition, white and black women comprised about equal percentages of recipients (meanings whites were statistically underrepresented and blacks were overrepresented). Hispanic coverage grew rapidly during the 1980s, and by the mid-1990s, about 20 percent of the children covered by AFDC were Hispanic.[13]

LEAVING WELFARE

Through most of the 1990s, the length of time that recipients received AFDC benefits tended to fall into three categories nearly equal in size: a short-term group received benefits for less than 1 year, a middle-length group collected AFDC payments for 1 to 3 years, and a long-term group received benefits for more than 3 years. (The median of the latter group was about 6 years.) The families with longer benefit episodes also tended, once they left AFDC rolls, to return more frequently. From Health and Human Services records and from several longitudinal surveys, we know that overall return rates were between about 40 percent and 42 percent. However, recidivism variations among different groups were so pronounced that the average was not very meaningful.

The best pictures of welfare recidivism are provided by two well-done studies that analyzed different longitudinal surveys, but reached a number of congruent findings. The first study, reported by Kathleen Harris, included nearly 600 women who were part of the Panel Study of Income Dynamics (PSID). In 1983 all of them lived with a child under age 18 and had received AFDC as a single mother. Harris followed their subsequent welfare utilization over the next six years.[14] The second study, reported by Gary Sandefur, relied upon data from the NLSY. This sample contained over 1,200 women who had ever received AFDC and were between the ages of 14 and 21 years in 1979. He followed their subsequent welfare use until 1993, when they were between 28 and 35 years of age.[15]

Both studies found that the length of welfare exits was about evenly divided into short-term and long-term periods, using two years as the dividing point. The more formal education a woman completed, the fewer the children she had, and the better the local job market where she lived, the more likely she would leave AFDC, and the greater the probability it would be a long-term exit. Women left the rolls for a variety of reasons: they married, found work, children's fathers resumed child-support payments, and so forth. Why they left did not appear to make much difference in recidivism rates. However, when Harris reexamined the women who left the rolls because of marriage (or cohabitation), she found that an important difference was whether her partner had a job. If so, the chance of the woman returning to welfare was reduced by 69 percent. Further, the women who exited welfare through marriage to a partner who was working were found later to be the economically most secure of the former welfare recipients. They had the lowest poverty rates and were most likely to pursue additional education, which improved their job prospects and thereby contributed to their economic security.[16]

A difference between the two studies involving race requires some reconciliation. In Sandefur's sample, black women had significantly fewer and shorter AFDC exits, and people in cities had fewer exits, but the possibility that the urban effect might be due to chance could not be ruled out. By contrast, Harris found the reverse: people who lived in cities had significantly fewer exits, and while black women had higher recidivism rates than whites, this difference could have been due to chance. Put together, what these findings *may* mean is that people who live in cities are disadvantaged with respect to leaving welfare, and given typical patterns of racial segregation, blacks predominate in many cities, though there are regional variations. Whether any study's conclusion attributes greater recidivism to race or to place of residence may therefore depend upon racial compositions in the particular mix of cities that is included in its sample.

Another possibility is that the effect of race upon AFDC recidivism depends (at least in part) upon other conditions. For example, in a study of almost 1,000 AFDC recipients in the state of Tennessee, Mwangi Kimenyi found that blacks were less likely than whites to leave welfare rolls when his analyses did not take into account the ratio of males to females. When he held this measure of the male marriageable pool constant, most of the racial difference disappeared, though blacks were then slightly more likely than whites to exit from welfare.[17] So perhaps it is women in cities who have the most difficulty leaving welfare, and perhaps the reason is that their chances of finding a partner with a job are dismal; and the fact is that the women living in these cities are typically black.

Without a working partner, it may be too difficult for most AFDC recipients to make enough money to voluntarily leave the welfare rolls, because the employment available to most of them pays a very low wage. All of the studies indicate that the local job market or local wage rates relative to AFDC benefits critically affect welfare exits. Some relevant figures are provided by Kathryn Edin's analysis of single mothers who were either AFDC recipients or low-wage workers in four major U.S. cities around the nation.[18] She compared both groups' total costs (for housing, food, clothing, transportation, etc.), and their total income (from wages or AFDC, food stamps, etc.) and found that in both groups expenses exceeded income. Most of the women had to resort to precarious means to supplement their monthly income: covert payments from absent fathers or boyfriends, shoplifting, working off the books or under false identities, and so forth.[19] On average, the welfare recipients had to make up a shortfall of $311 per month. That was the difference between the value of all their welfare benefits and their costs. By comparison, a main job, second job, and overtime left the low-wage women an average of $441 short of meeting their families' monthly expenses. Edin calculated that for single mothers receiving AFDC, food stamps, housing subsidies, and so on to duplicate their economic situation off of welfare they would need jobs that paid them about $16,000 per year.[20] (The poverty threshold for a family of four in 1995 was $15,569.[21])

In sum, Edin's analysis suggested that living on welfare was not really a very good deal. Life was even worse for one-parent families with low-wage jobs, though. Given the limited education and work experience of most of these women, jobs in the "$5-an-hour-ghetto" were the best they could expect, but that was not enough to entice most of them off the welfare rolls.[22]

TRADITIONAL WELFARE'S CRITICS

Since their inception, ADC, Food Stamps, and related government benefits that can be received by unmarried women with children have been singled out for special criticism, out of proportion to their relatively small cost. We will examine those criticisms in detail. First let us acknowledge that there is some arbitrariness to singling out this one set of benefits and labeling them welfare, but not applying the pejorative label to other (even more expensive) programs where it could just as easily fit. For example, in 1995 the Senate and House debated welfare reform, which they equated with the elimination or reduction of AFDC, Food Stamps, SSI, and Medicaid. Almost no one mentioned the other 125 programs in the federal budget that provided grants or subsidies to private businesses: direct payments to farmers growing wheat, rice, and cotton ($9.8 billion in FY95); subsidized air-traffic services to airlines and private-plane owners ($8.7 billion in FY95).[23]

Equating welfare with benefits to poor and powerless recipients and criticizing welfare's consequences for these beneficiaries began in earnest when Nixon replaced Johnson as president in 1968.[24] Nixon and his advisors regarded ADC and recently enacted programs such as SSI and Food Stamps as promoting immorality and a lack of discipline. The new administration claimed that government benefits encouraged sexually promiscuous behavior without concern for consequences. For example, Nixon's policy advisor (later a senator) Daniel Patrick Moynihan described the Great Society as having been a major contributor to the destruction of the traditional American family.[25]

To be more specific, it is not so much welfare per se that has drawn the critics' ire, but benefit programs that are regarded as having encouraged nonmarital childrearing. For example, as analyzed by sociologist David Popenoe, "AFDC treats having a child out of wedlock as—in effect—a favored lifestyle that is deliberately subsidized by the government."[26]

One of the most outspoken and influential critics of traditional welfare has been Charles Murray. When he testified before the Senate Finance Committee in 1995, he insisted that reducing nonmarital births was "the prerequisite for rebuilding civic life in low-income black America and preventing a slide into chaos in white America."[27] The children of poor, unmarried mothers are neglected, malnurtured, and ill prepared to be parents themselves. But, who can help them? Extended families are eroded by nonmarital childbearing, and neighborhood institutions have broken down in the communities in which many of these families live. So, Murray continued, with each generation that grows up in welfare homes, the problem gets worse. And job training programs for welfare mothers are not the answer because they do not address the most pressing problem: these children will still be raised by incompetent mothers in fatherless homes.

In a former best-seller, *The Bell Curve*, coauthored by Murray, he and Richard Herrnstein theorized that the smarter a (single) woman was, the more likely she would think about the consequences of sexual intercourse and act accordingly in order not to become an unwed mother. The least intelligent women acted thoughtlessly and impulsively. Therefore, the co-authors hypothesized, women with low intelligence are more likely to have out-of-wedlock births. Reexamining data from the National Longitudinal Study of Youth, they reported that women in the top intelligence quartile almost always had their children nine months or more after marrying; but fewer than one-half of the women in the lowest IQ group conceived in a marital relationship. Further, the effects of IQ appeared to be independent of the woman's formal education and socioeconomic background. Because young women who are poor but bright are getting scholarships, they defer childbearing. Poor young women who are dull "have nothing else to do, and so have a baby."[28] By supporting such thoughtless actions, they conclude, AFDC has contributed to a deterioration of the overall intelligence in the society.

Many readers found *The Bell Curve*'s assertions too vindictive, and blind to the possibility that some unmarried women might have positive reasons for wanting children. From our examination of the steps leading to out-of-wedlock births (in chapter 3), we know that all women do not simply back into unwed motherhood. In addition, Herrnstein and Murray's analyses and conclusions have been seriously challenged on methodological grounds.[29] However, let us continue to follow Murray's argument because most pertinent to us is his thesis that welfare has been a (if not the) major cause of the increase in out-of-wedlock births. Therefore, once AFDC and related benefits are terminated, he has predicted, nonmarital birthrates will soon fall.

A number of social researchers have tried to estimate the relationship between welfare benefits and out-of-wedlock rates and ratios. As part of the *Report to Congress* issued by the Department of Health and Human Services, Robert Moffitt summarized the results of nineteen studies reported between 1970 and 1995. Most of them were designed to test the rational choice hypothesis that if welfare acts as an inducement to women to have nonmarital births, then the greater the size of the benefit offered in a state, the higher will be the out-of-wedlock rate in that state. About one-half of the studies summarized by Moffitt concluded that the size of welfare benefits increased nonmarital childbearing among whites. About one-third had the same finding for nonwhites.[30]

Most of the studies that found any welfare effect reported that it was small in magnitude. Even Murray conceded that these studies indicated that cutting welfare benefits would lead to a very small reduction in nonmarital childbearing, but he contended that the studies had been done incorrectly. One problem shared by most of them was an exclusive reliance upon AFDC. To equate its cash payment with welfare ignores the value of food stamps, Medicaid, and so forth. When the size of AFDC payments is the sole indicator of a state's benefits, measurement errors will result because some states with relatively low AFDC payments offer relatively high benefit packages. In addition, Murray argues, looking for differences across states ignores the fact that welfare went up everywhere. Its main effect on nonmarital births was due to the national change in benefits, and that overwhelmed variations among states, making the latter unimportant.[31]

However, if one tracks the overall number of welfare recipients in the nation and compares that to fluctuations in the size of average family welfare benefits, as we have done earlier in this chapter, it is very difficult to see anything like what Murray envisioned. If anything, benefits (in constant dollars) tended to contract during those periods in which the number of recipients expanded.[32]

Particularly disquieting to Murray's theory was the fact that most studies did not find a correlation between welfare benefits and out-of-wedlock rates among blacks. Given the large contribution of blacks to overall out-of-wedlock rates, the absence of a welfare effect in this group was very damaging to his theory. This prompted Murray to devise a new out-of-wedlock incidence measure. Unlike conventional out-of-wedlock rates, which focus upon nonmarital births per 1,000 *single* women, his new measure calculates nonmarital births per 1,000 women, *married or not*. This new measure is designed, Murray states, to describe out-of-wedlock production per unit of population. Among blacks he found that variations in this incidence measure seemed dependent upon the value of welfare benefits. For example, sharp increases in each year's benefits in the late 1960s were followed, two years later, by marked increases in Murray's out-of-wedlock incidence measure. When blacks were viewed with this new measure, he concluded, "marriage and out-of-wedlock childbearing . . . behaved exactly as one would predict if one expected welfare to discourage women from getting married and induce single women to have babies."[33]

Combining married and unmarried black women in a single measure produced the result Murray was seeking primarily because the percentage of black women who were married was shrinking. Between 1975 and 1992, for example, the out-of-wedlock ratio increased from about 48 per 1,000 newborns to almost 69 per 1,000. Decomposing the variables that accounted for this increase discloses that reductions in the percentage of women who were married was the main factor, accounting for nearly 60 percent of the overall increase in blacks' out-of-wedlock ratios. During the same time period, a declining percentage of married women made a significant contribution to the increase in whites' out-of-wedlock ratios, but an increase in nonmarital fertility was nearly twice as important among nonwhites.[34]

In other words, the fertility of unmarried black women increased between 1975 and 1992, but not all that dramatically; what changed most was that there were a lot more of them. This again takes us back to the question of why black women were marrying at lower rates. Murray's answer is apparently that after calculating their alternatives, they opted out of marriage in order to bear out-of-wedlock children and be eligible for welfare benefits. However, this would not be a rational economic strategy for women to follow if they could find men with jobs. Then it would be economically advantageous for women to defer childbearing until after they were married because marital births are associated with higher family incomes, especially when both husband and wife are working.

And in terms of people's values, marriage is clearly the option most people would prefer. Nearly three-quarters of the adult U.S. population agrees that "people who want children ought to get married," a small percentage have not yet made up their minds, and only 15 percent disagree.[35] Thus, as we saw in every place we have examined in this book, people overwhelmingly consider marriage the ideal arrangement, especially when children are involved. The key question, again, is: What prevents them from acting in accordance with their preferences? (We will return to this question at the very end of this chapter.)

WELFARE REFORM

Even before the Great Society's expansion of benefits, a few states in the 1950s responded to the increased cost of ADC and the changes in the beneficiaries' race and marital status by trying to exclude unmarried mothers and their children from ADC coverage. Some states tried to insist that eligibility required that mothers accept employment if "suitable arrangements" could be found for their children. However, local and state officials were able to restrict benefits only sporadically, because the limiting conditions they tried to impose proved elusive. For example, a day-care center provides a "suitable arrangement" for children of what age?[36]

Coming to office directly after Johnson transformed America with the Great Society, Nixon would have liked to dismantle many of the new programs, but he was thwarted by Democratic majorities in Congress, and then diverted by Vietnam War protests in the 1970s. The first real changes began when Reagan became president. First elected in 1982, he called for an overhaul of welfare and proposed that states be given more leeway to design their own welfare-to-work experiments. Aid to Families with Dependent Children had covered an unchanging number of families over the previous fifteen years, but there had also been fifteen years of evaluation research that examined the costs and benefits of job-search programs, education and training programs, and so forth. Legislative leaders, the governors' association, and others quoted from that group of the studies, which showed it was possible to place welfare recipients in jobs and that there would be net government savings, even if the government had to pay for job training. Almost no one touted the substantial number of studies that did not concur in these projections.[37]

During Reagan's second term, with bipartisan support, he signed the Family Support Act in 1988. It mandated states to place recipients of AFDC into jobs or job training, but by the end of Reagan's second term, over 70 percent of AFDC recipients were neither employed nor in training. The act also ordered states to collect more vigorously child-support payments, but enforcement remained very sporadic. Further, the act's principal objective, to reduce welfare recipients, was entirely offset by a recession in 1990, which helped to drive up the number of families receiving AFDC and related assistance. The rolls increased rapidly until late in 1992, when Reagan's second term ended and Democrat Clinton became president. Among the new president's highest priorities was a complete overhaul of welfare, an objective historically associated more with Republicans than with Democrats. However, Clinton was governor of Arkansas when Reagan proposed the Family Support Act, and Clinton strongly endorsed it when he presided over the Association of State Governors.

As candidate and as president, Clinton promised to "end welfare as we know it," and the Republican Congress shared this objective. However, he considered the cuts initially proposed by the Republican-controlled Congress too draconian. The House plan included sharp cutbacks or the elimination of: AFDC, SSI, Food Stamps, and Medicaid. In the view of House Speaker Newt Gingrich, the 1960s Great Society started the nation off on the wrong foot, and government programs compounded the mistake over the next thirty years. "We are committed to welfare reform because what we are doing to the poor in America is destructive and immoral," he said.[38] An important part of his correction involved targeting benefits that had been paid to women who had out-of-wedlock births. For example, the House proposal would have ended all AFDC payments to unmarried women under age 18.

While Clinton and the Congress negotiated over what to cut and by how much, states were encouraged to seek waivers that would enable them to modify traditional welfare benefits and still receive federal reimbursement. Florida, Massachusetts, and Wisconsin were among the first of a number of states to try to establish work obligations in place of AFDC payments. The governor of Massachusetts explained the logic underlying most of these states' plans: "People will never lift themselves out of poverty if they are stuck on welfare."[39]

It was not until the end of Clinton's first term that he and the Congress compromised on the Welfare Reform Bill passed in 1996. It is impossible (as this book is being written) to say how this bill will eventually affect various benefits, because some features of the new law will not be implemented until after the year 2000, and they may be changed before then. In addition, the effects of some of the law's new eligibility criteria have not yet been resolved. During the first year, for example, over one-half of the children receiving SSI payments whose cases were reviewed were terminated. Nearly 85 percent of those who were cut off had been classified as having "mental disorders," which included: retardation, learning disabilities, personality disorders, and behavioral problems. Some congressional critics contended that Social Security administrators were employing stricter standards than the law required, but it is still far from clear how such cases will ultimately be resolved.[40]

Under the 1996 law, the federal government is also giving block grants to the states, and the states have much more leeway in deciding how to allocate benefits. Thus the federal government no longer reimburses states for a set percentage of the costs of specific programs, such as AFDC or Emergency Assistance. Instead, states now receive a Temporary Assistance to Needy Families (TANF) block grant. How each state will choose to allocate benefits is yet to be determined. What we can now say overall with certainty is that (1) states will have to move large numbers of current AFDC and related program recipients into the workforce, and that (2) the block grants will not permit states to maintain the same array of welfare benefits that grew out of the Great Society.[41]

OUT-OF-WEDLOCK REDUCTION PLANS

The Welfare Reform Bill of 1996 put up some additional federal funds to serve as inducements to the states to design new ventures that would specifically target nonmarital birthrates. Again, it will be some years before the effectiveness of the new programs can really be assessed. However, we can describe their objectives and offer some preliminary estimates of the likely impact.

The Department of Health and Human Services will offer bonuses of at least $20 million to each of the five states that show the greatest two-year drop in out-of-wedlock births. The meter began running for this "contest" when the bill was signed in 1997. The idea is that in response to these incentives, some states will be innovative, and as the laggard states see others cutting their welfare rolls, they will try to emulate the strategies that seem to work.[42] States are implementing a variety of plans, some of which seem based upon reasonable assumptions, and some of which do not. In Maryland, for example, officials are seeking the federal bonus by designing after-school programs for teenage girls who might otherwise be home alone.[43] Especially if combined with prosecution of "predatory older men," as urged by the Senate, such programs could help to reduce that percentage of out-of-wedlock conceptions that was consistently seen in prior chapters to have a coercive element. In Michigan, by contrast, officials are counting on a program that will prevent teenage fathers from participating in high-school sports unless they make child-support payments. The underlying assumption here is questionable: are there any data to suggest that high-school athletes father a significant number of out-of-wedlock children or that they could support them if their eligibility was in the balance?

One catch in the out-of-wedlock reduction contest is that a state's cutback during the two-year period cannot be accomplished by greater reliance upon induced abortions. Specifically, to be eligible for the bonus money, the rate of abortion in the state after 1997 cannot exceed the state's rate in 1995.

Further narrowing the options states can afford to pursue is another federal program that provides each state $1 million per year, for five years, to pay for sex education that advocates only abstinence. If states want to promote any other means of preventing births, they must pay for it themselves. Most states are taking the federal money (grumbling in some cases) and teaching abstinence to elementary-school children or promoting it in media campaigns outside of schools. In metropolitan Washington, D.C., for example, billboards state "VIRGIN" in large, red letters and underneath, in smaller black letters, add, "Teach your kid it's not a dirty word."[44]

Sociologist Norval Glenn believes that concerted efforts to change young people's outlooks are beginning to bear fruit. From an inspection of attitude surveys over the past thirty years, he discerned a small recent move among high-school seniors toward more conservative values regarding nonmarital sex and out-of-wedlock births. He thinks efforts to change young people's values should continue to be given high priority. Few young people are so alienated, he observes, as to be indifferent to "normative cues" from institutions such as government and schools. These cues, beginning in the 1960s, were ambiguous with respect to nonmarital sex and childbearing. To reverse the trends of the last thirty years, he argues, requires that the right cultural message be conveyed to young people.45

How this is done, I think, will make all the difference. In the preceding chapter, I argued that abstract values by themselves were not generally very likely to influence behavior strongly, and we reviewed supportive data showing the importance of intervening circumstances in swaying people's actions. There are congruent findings among the very few direct studies of abstinence. Russell Eisenman, for example, reported that abstinence values could be imparted in programs, but the effects of these values upon students' behavior were very uncertain.46 Thus, rather than encourage virginity on a billboard, it might be more effective to teach young people the kinds of concrete situations to avoid if they want to remain sexually abstinent or else to fund abstinence support groups.

Such groups have formed in recent years, sometimes in unlikely places, such as an inner-city high school in Jersey City, New Jersey. A social worker in the school, who does not think teenagers should be sexually active, identified a group of girls who were virgins and brought them together. They met every few weeks to reaffirm their commitment to abstain from sexual intercourse and to discuss the difficulties each experienced in maintaining her commitment. For example, one slim 14-year-old girl explained, with embarrassed giggles, how her 16-year-old boy friend kept pressuring her to be intimate. She recounted that she finally told him he would have to respect her desire to remain a virgin or else end the relationship. (He chose the second option.) The other ten girls around the table clapped and yelled, "Go, girl."47

In conclusion, it is difficult to imagine any of the programs now underway making more than a very modest contribution to reducing out-of-wedlock births. The problem is that they nibble around the margins of the problem rather than addressing the primary underlying predicament. A very impressive body of evidence can be marshalled attesting to the importance of the shrinking male marriageable pool in driving up out-of-wedlock births, but little attention is being directed at solutions to this core problem.

At the end of the preceding chapter, we summarized our descriptions of other places and times, concluding that male joblessness seemed consistently to be the beginning of a chain leading to higher out-of-wedlock ratios. In this chapter, where our focus shifted to welfare, we have found that a shortage of marriageable men seemed to be the most important variable in leading single mothers to traditional welfare and that marriage to a working partner seemed to be the most permanent means for single mothers to permanently leave traditional welfare.

Unfortunately, in my opinion, welfare reform has consistently gone for the "quick fix." Just get single mothers off the rolls, they seem to say, do not worry too much about what happens to their children, and we can call it the family values solution! Not addressed is the underlying challenge, namely, to discourage single motherhood in favor of married, two-parent families. The question that should be at the top of the list is, What can government do to encourage the formation of two-parent families and to strengthen those that exist? One important part of the answer must surely entail deliberately expanded work opportunities for hard-to-place male workers. That is the only practical way to make them more attractive to potential mates, both as husbands and fathers, and thereby break the chain that begins with a constricted male marriage-able pool and ends with out-of-wedlock births.

NOTES

1. Parents' welfare use also has an intergenerational impact even when economic conditions are held constant. For further discussion of poverty and welfare use, see Mark R. Rank and Li-Chen Cheng, "Welfare Use across Generations," *Journal of Marriage and the Family*, 57, Aug. 1995.

2. Committee on Ways and Means, *Overview of Entitlement Programs: Green Book* (Washington, DC: U.S. House of Representatives, 1994), p. 2.

3. U.S. Department of Health and Human Services, *Characteristics and Financial Circumstances of AFDC Recipients: FY 1993,* Office of Family Assistance (Washington, DC: GPO, 1995), table 15.

4. Sandra K. Danziger and Kelleen Kaye, "Trends in Welfare Receipt and Nonmarital Births" (paper presented at meetings of American Sociological Association. 1996), table 1.

5. For further discussion, see especially chapter 2 in Mary Jo Bane and David T. Ellwood (Eds.), *Welfare Realities* (Cambridge, MA: Harvard University Press, 1994).

6. See Mary Ellen Richmond, *Marriage and the State* (New York: Russell Sage Foundation, 1929). Richmond, who died in 1928, directed charitable organizations that served unwed mothers in several cities. She also established a casework training program that evolved into the Columbia School of Social Work.

7. For further discussion of the origins of these and related plans, see Theda Skocpol, *Protecting Soldiers and Mothers* (Cambridge, MA: Harvard University Press, 1992), and Linda Gordon, *Pitied but Not Entitled* (New York: Free Press, 1994), p. 51.

8. George Liebmann, "Back to the Maternity Home," *American Enterprise*, 6, Jan./Feb. 1995, p. 51.

9. For further discussion of race and gender differences, see Joya Misra and Frances Akins, "The Welfare State and Women" (paper presented at American Sociological Association Meetings August 1996). For more on the origins of ADC and state differences, see Nancy K. Cauthen and Edwin Amenta, "Not for Widows Only," *American Sociological Review*, 61, June 1996.

10. However, 70 percent of Medicaid expenses went to the aged or disabled. See Carolyn L. Weaver, "Welfare Payments to the Disabled," *American Enterprise*, 6, Jan./Feb. 1995.

11. U.S. Department of Health and Human Services, *Characteristics and Financial Circumstances of AFDC Recipients, FY 96*. Administration for Children and Families (Washington, DC: GPO, 1997), pp. 1–2.

12. The above figures showing trends in the value of AFDC benefits are taken from table 2 in Danzinger and Kaye. For further discussion of welfare packages, see Roberta Spalter-Roth, Beverly Burr, Heidi Hartmann, and Lois Shaw, *Welfare that Works: The Working Lives of AFDC Recipients* (Washington, DC: Institute for Women's Policy Research, 1995).

13. *Characteristics and Financial Circumstances of AFDC Recipients, FY 1996*, table 17.

14. Kathleen M. Harris, "Life after Welfare," *American Sociological Review*, 61, June 1996.

15. Gary D. Sandefur, "Is Welfare A Trap?" (paper presented at meetings of the American Sociological Association, August 1995).

16. Harris.

17. Mwangi S. Kimenyi, "Rational Choice, Culture of Poverty, and the Intergenerational Transmission of Welfare Dependency," *Southern Economic Journal*, 57, April 1991.

18. Kathryn J. Edin, "The Myths of Dependence and Self-Sufficiency," *Focus*, 17, Fall/Winter 1995. See also Edin and Laura Lein, *Making Ends Meet* (New York: Russell Sage Foundation, 1996).

19. Danziger and Koussoudji describe similar attempts by former General Assistance recipients to raise "risky" cash by begging, selling blood, collecting refundable cans and bottles, and so forth. See Sandra K. Danziger and Sherrie A. Kossoudji, "When Welfare Ends" (Unpublished project report, School of Social Work, University of Michigan, 1995).

20. Edin, p. 8.

21. This figure assumes a cash income and is adjusted annually using the Consumer Price Index. See the Appendix in United States General Accounting Office, *Poverty Measurement*, Health, Education and Human Services Division (Washington, DC: United States General Accounting Office, 1997).

22. For an analysis of the limited earning capacity of women receiving welfare, see Gary Burtless, "Employment Prospects of Welfare Recipients," in Demetra S. Nightingale and Robert H. Haveman (Eds.), *The Work Alternative* (Washington, DC: Urban Institute Press, 1995).

23. See "Business Welfare," in *American Enterprise*, 6, July/August 1995, pp. 82–83.

24. For an analysis that focuses upon the role of racial animosities in Nixon's reactions to these programs, see Jill Quadagno, *The Color of Welfare* (New York: Oxford University Press, 1994).

25. Daniel Patrick Moynihan, "How the Great Society Destroyed the American Family," *Public Interest*, Summer 1992. For an overview, see also Amy T. Schalet, "Civilized or Stigmatized?" (paper presented at meeting of American Sociological Association, 1996).

26. David Popenoe, "Family Caps," *Society*, 33, July/August 1996, p. 26.

27. Charles Murray, "Keeping Priorities Straight on Welfare Reform," *Society*, 33, July/Aug. 1996, p. 10.

28. Richard J. Herrnstein and Charles Murray, *The Bell Curve* (New York: Free Press, 1994), p. 190. They prefer to use the term "illegitimacy," following Malinowski (see chapter 1), and insist that in the long run it will prove to be the best term.

29. See, for example, Steven Jay Gould, "Mismeasure by Any Measure," in Russell Jacoby and Naomi Glauberman (Eds.), *The Bell Curve Debate* (New York: Times Books, 1995).

30. Robert A. Moffitt, "The Effect of the Welfare System on Nonmarital Childbearing," in U.S. Department of Health and Human Services, *Report to Congress on Out-of-Wedlock Childbearing* (Washington, DC: GPO, 1995).

31. Charles Murray, "Does Welfare Bring More Babies?" *American Enterprise*, 5, Jan./Feb. 1994. Other critics add that AFDC did not operate alone at the national level. During the 1960s changes in federal tax policies created a "marriage penalty" in which traditional families lost relative advantages to divorced and unmarried parents. See Allan Carlson, "Family Questions," *Society*, 27, July/Aug. 1990.

32. Murray has two counterresponses to the contradictory data: (1) the woman in the street did not realize that the real value of benefits was declining because she saw her friends' welfare checks getting larger each year, and (2) recognizing that welfare is not a good deal takes more intelligence than most of them have. It seems inconsistent for Murray to pursue either of these arguments, though, because both take him away from the rational choice underpinnings of his theory.

33. Murray, "Does Welfare Bring More Babies?" p. 59.

34. Data from Herbert L. Smith, S. Philip Morgan, and Tanya Koropecki-Cox, "A Decomposition of Trends in the Nonmarital Fertility

Rates of Blacks and Whites in the U.S., 1960–1992." *Demography*, 33, May 1996.

35. National Opinion Research Center, May 1994. Reported in "Opinion Pulse," *American Enterprise*, 6, July/Aug. 1995, p. 102.

36. For an analysis of changes during the 1950s, see Yvonne Zylan, "Constructing the Patriarchal Welfare State" (paper presented at meetings of the American Sociological Association, 1994), and Sarah A. Soule and Yvonne Zylan, "Runaway Train" (paper presented at meetings of the American Sociological Association, 1996).

37. For further discussion of the role of evaluation research in the welfare reform of 1988, see Stacey J. Oliker, "Does Welfare Work?" *Social Problems*, 41, May 1994.

38. Quoted in *New York Times*, December 3, 1995, Section 4, p. 1.

39. Quuoted in *American Enterprise*, 5, July/Aug. 1994. p. 14.

40. *New York Times*, August 15, 1997, p. A28.

41. For further details of the impact upon states, see Jocelyn Guyer, *State Funding Requirements under the New Welfare Law*, Washington, DC: Center on Budget and Policy Priorities, April 15, 1997.

42. For further discussion of how the "administrative culture" is expected to change, see chapter 1 in Bane and Ellwood.

43. Several states' plans are described in Jon Jeter, "Births and the Nation," *Washington Post National Weekly*, Sept. 16–22, 1996.

44. *New York Times*, July 23, 1997, p. A19.

45. Norval D. Glenn, "Welfare Experimentation," *Society*, 33, July/Aug. 1996.

46. Russell Eisenman, "Conservative Sexual Values," *Journal of Sex Education and Therapy*, 20, Feb. 1994.

47. *New York Times*, Aug. 7, 1997, p. B1.

Suggestions for Further Reading

Bane, Mary Jo, and David T. Ellwood (Eds.). *Welfare Realities*. Cambridge, MA: Harvard University Press, 1994.

Blankenhorn, David. *Fatherless America*. New York: Basic Books, 1995.

Bolles, A. Lynn. *Sister Jamaica*. Lanham, MD: University Press of America, 1996.

Cherlin, Andrew. *Marriage, Divorce and Remarriage*. Cambridge, MA: Harvard University Press, 1992.

Coltrane, Scott. *Family Man*. New York: Oxford University Press, 1996.

Evason, Eileen, and Roberta Woods. *Poverty, Charity and "Doing the Double."* Brookfield, VT: Ashgate, 1995.

Friedlander, Daniel, and Gary Burtless. *Five Years After*. New York: Russell Sage, 1995.

Gerson, Kathleen. *No Man's Land*. New York: Basic Books, 1993.

Gilbert, Neil. *Welfare Justice*. New Haven, CT: Yale University Press, 1995.

Gordon, Linda. *Pitied but Not Entitled*. New York: Free Press, 1994.

Herrnstein, Richard J., and Charles Murray. *The Bell Curve*. New York: Free Press, 1994.

Koven, Seth, and Sonya Michel (Eds.). *Mothers of a New World*. New York: Routledge, 1993.

Laslett, Peter, Karla Oosterveen, and Richard M. Smith (Eds). *Bastardy and Its Comparative History*. Cambridge, MA: Harvard University Press, 1980.

Luker, Kristen. *Dubious Conceptions*. Cambridge, MA: Harvard University Press, 1996.

McLanahan, Sara, and Gary Sandefur. *Growing Up with a Single Parent*. Cambridge, MA: Harvard University Press, 1994.

Mason, Mary A., Arlene Skolnick, and Stephen D. Sugerman. *All Our Families.* New York: Oxford University Press, 1998.

Mink, Gwendolyn. *The Ways of Motherhood.* Ithaca, NY: Cornell University Press, 1995.

Moore, Kristin A., Brent C. Miller, and Donna R. Morrison. *Adolescent Sex, Contraception and Childbearing.* Washington, DC: Child Trends, 1995.

Popenoe, David. *Life without Father.* New York: Free Press, 1996.

Quadagno, Jill. *The Color of Welfare.* New York: Oxford University Press, 1994.

Rank, Mark A. *Living on the Edge.* New York: Columbia University Press, 1994.

Sherwood Joan., *Poverty in Eighteenth-Century Spain.* Toronto: University of Toronto Press, 1988.

Skocpol, Theda. *Protecting Soldiers and Mothers.* Cambridge, MA: Harvard University Press, 1992.

U.S. Department of Health and Human Services. *Report to Congress on Out-of-Wedlock Childbearing.* Washington, DC: Government Printing Office (GPO), 1995.

Wilson, William J. *When Work Disappears.* New York: Knopf, 1996.

Index

About the Author

MARK ABRAHAMSON is Professor of Sociology at the University of Connecticut. For more than 20 years, he has combined scholarly and administrative activities at the university—having served as Department Head, Dean, and Associate Vice President for Academic Affairs. He is the author of a dozen books and more than 30 articles, and is also a former Program Director at the National Science Foundation.

ISBN 0-275-95662-8

90000>

9 780275 956622

HARDCOVER BAR CODE